Wallace-Homestead

price guide to
DOLLS

Robert W. Miller

Published by

WH books

Wallace-Homestead Book Company
1912 Grand Avenue
Des Moines, Iowa 50305

*Library of Congress
Catalog Card No. 79-63081
ISBN: 0-87069-269-0*

Back cover photograph: VIOLA (twins) — bisque socket head marked 4500 N$_T$, S — five pointed star with PB in center — H, original mohair wig, open mouth, sleep eyes, composition/wood jointed body. 21″ tall. **$250-300 each.**

Cover photograph: left, JUMEAU bisque socket head marked DEPOSE TETE JUMEAU Bte. S.D.G.D. 7 (red checkmarks); human hair wig, pierced ears, blue paperweight eyes, closed mouth, mache/wood jointed body marked BEBE JUMEAU DIPLOME d'HONNEUR. 17″ tall. **$1,800-1,900.** Center: K (star) R SIMON HALBIG bisque socket head marked K (star) R SIMON HALBIG 126 1.2; human hair wig, flirty eyes, open mouth, composition body, tremble tongue. 20″ tall, 13″ head circumference. **$550-600.** Right: E D bisque socket head marked E 8 D (incised), Jumeau checkmarks, human hair wig, brown paperweight eyes, closed mouth, wood/mache jointed body. 20″ tall. **$1,300-1,450.** Teddy Bear has swivel head, tan pads on feet; black, stitched-on nose, jointed shoulders and hips, button eyes. 15″ tall. **$65-80.**

2

TABLE OF CONTENTS

EDITORIAL NOTE: Accent marks and symbols denoting foreign sounds are omitted in the text of this book because of lack of flexibility in modern electronic typesetting.

Acknowledgments

A lot of folks helped make the first edition of the WALLACE-HOMESTEAD PRICE GUIDE TO DOLLS possible. As a great many choose to remain anonymous, I can only say that those who were in on the beginning know how I feel toward them.

This second edition is complete with a new color section, new front cover, and, most important, up-to-date prices compiled by authorities in the field of dollology. A special thanks is due to a kind and lovely lady, Catherine Arehart, a doll authority in her own right. We all could take a page from her Book of Life.

To photographer Andrew Thurman, "Well done!" Clear and concise photographs are absolutely necessary, and, as you can readily see, the new color section is a quality job. We also thank Andrew's associate.

Whether you're just a beginner or consider yourself an authority on dolls, this WALLACE-HOMESTEAD PRICE GUIDE TO DOLLS is for YOU! Visit the doll museums listed by state locations on page 212. Subscribe to the fine doll publications noted on page 212, but most of all, enjoy collecting dolls.

Hope you enjoy using this price guide as much as I enjoyed putting it together for YOU.

Introduction

This WALLACE-HOMESTEAD PRICE GUIDE TO DOLLS, published periodically, is recognized as the leader in the field of pricing dolls and has been for the past six years.

Accepted overwhelmingly by dealers, collectors, museums, and appraisers, it never-the-less does not claim to be the final authority. But, the prices herein have been established by experts and are accepted as the retail values for dolls in excellent condition at the time of this publication.

Obviously, as time passes, it is imperative to update your collection accordingly. Since the collecting of dolls is one of the fastest growing hobbies in the world, sharp price increases are to be expected, especially at auctions. Use common sense! Do you really want it? Do you really need it?

This WALLACE-HOMESTEAD PRICE GUIDE TO DOLLS is the only price guide that gives you a Chronology of Dolls, a Glossary of Doll Terms, the location of doll/toy museums in the United States and Canada, a **full** color section, names and addresses of all the doll publications, and the names and addresses of the most popular antiques and collectibles publications.

Only this WALLACE-HOMESTEAD PRICE GUIDE TO DOLLS is the **Complete** price guide. Compare it with the others; see for yourself.

Although every effort has been made to eliminate errors, the editor and the publisher cannot be held responsible for mistakes, either in typography or judgment, in the prices given herein. Thank you!

CHRONOLOGY OF DOLLS

Rather than present a chronology of dolls as a whole, we will consider here the dolls found in this Price Guide, most of which are available to collectors. By giving a range of dates in each of the categories of materials in which the various types of dolls were produced, we hope to help the novice collector in determining the date of a particular doll.

The collector must realize that certain companies produced the same type of doll over a period of several years, so it is nearly impossible to precisely date a doll. In some cases excellent documentation is available, and therefore a doll can be dated more accurately.

ALL-BISQUE

All-bisque dolls were produced from the 1850s through World War II. Germany and France were the leading producers, with Japan contributing a larger proportion of dolls in this field during World War I.

Usually all-bisque dolls are small, the largest ones not exceeding 12 inches. The Rose O'Neill Kewpies proved to be the most popular.

AMERICAN BISQUE

Although several companies made bisque-head dolls, the Fulper Pottery Company is the only one represented here. They made bisque heads for dolls and a few all-bisque dolls from 1918-1921.

CELLULOID

Celluloid products were invented in 1869, but dolls did not appear in number until the 1880s. In the early 1900s several German firms produced celluloid heads for dolls. These continued to be popular until the 1920s to 1930s.

The Parsons-Jackson Company placed dolls made of Biskoline (a celluloid-type material) on the market in 1910. They were granted a patent on December 8, 1914, for the Parsons-Jackson baby doll, and production was continued for several years.

The outstanding company in celluloid production is the Rheinische Gummi & Celluloid Fabrik Company which has made celluloid heads for several companies since the 1880s and has continued production, including the Kathe Kruse dolls of the 1950s.

Japanese celluloid dolls were of slightly inferior quality but were produced in large quantities after World War I.

CHINA

Although the making of china dolls began around 1750, the majority found in collections today date from the 1830s and 1840s.

Master doll makers in Germany began making beautiful china-head dolls in the 1830s. The name "Biedermeier" has been given to the bald-head china doll with a wig. However, most of them were probably not made in this era. Those pictured in this book have the hair style of the 1830s. Although the molded-hair chinas reflect the hair styles fashionable in the 1840s through the 1870s, it must be remembered that dolls with these hair styles were produced for many years after they were first introduced. The date of each type of hair style is noted with each doll.

"Frozen Charlottes," often called pillar dolls, bathing babies, or solid china, date from the 1850s to the 1930s. Hair styles found on Frozen Charlottes, similar to the china-head dolls, date them in the same manner. "Frozen Charlie" is the name given to the Charlottes which have the boy hair style.

CLOTH

Cloth or rag dolls that could be cuddled have always been popular with children. Mothers have made them by hand for centuries. They were manufactured in England and France in the early 1800s, but makers in the United States took over the market in the last quarter of the century.

Izannah Walker of Central Falls, R.I., started making dolls with oil-painted features about 1885, but she didn't patent her method until November 4, 1873. Many of her dolls therefore are not marked.

Later (1890s and early 1900s) makers of this type of doll included the Columbian Doll by Emma Adams of Oswego, N.Y.; the Alabama Indestructible Doll by Ella Smith of Roanoke, Ala.; and the Chase dolls by Martha Chase of Pawtucket, R.I. Chase dolls of this type were made into the 1920s in a wide variety, including characters from *Alice in Wonderland* and the 1911 "hospital dolls."

The late 1890s and early 1900s brought a flood of printed cloth advertising dolls from several companies. Foremost among these are the Art Fabric Mills of New York, the Arnold Print Works of North Adams, Mass., and the Lawrence Company of Boston.

Margarete Steiff was making felt dolls before 1900 and produced large quantities of them in the early 1900s. Her trademark of "Button in Ear" is still in use today.

Kathe Kruse started making cloth dolls in 1910, and her dolls are also still on the market today. Though not of the same cloth type, they are still just as appealing.

All-felt Lenci dolls were produced in Italy by Di E. Scavinni in the 1920s.

Norah Wellings was a popular doll maker in England from the 1920s to the 1940s. Her dolls were made of velvet and are labeled on the foot.

COMPOSITION

Early composition was merely a change in the mixture combined to make papier-mache. Sawdust was substituted for paper, and the new material was called composition. This invention is attributed to Lazarus Reichman of New York City in 1877. It is from improvements on this process that the modern composition dolls are made. Since several source books on composition dolls are now in the market, we will give here only a few highlights on these collectible dolls.

Joseph Kallus made some of the early kewpies (1916) and formed the Cameo Doll Company in 1922, which continued producing Rose O'Neill kewpies and Scootles.

E. I. Horsman, in business in 1865, is famous for the now-rare Billikens, Baby Bumps, Campbell Kids, HEbee-SHEbee, and others.

American Character Doll Company made several mama dolls in the 1920s and 1930s.

Madame Alexander Doll Company, founded in 1923, procduced story book characters in 1930 and many personality dolls such as Princess Elizabeth, Mary Martin, Sonja Henie, Margaret O'Brien, Ann Shirley, and the Dionne Quints.

Ideal Toy Corporation, founded in 1902, began production of dolls in 1934 and made one of the biggest sellers in doll history, the Shirley Temple doll.

CRECHE

Due to the care these figures had over the ages, they date among the oldest dolls found in collections today. Though the sculpting of them began in the 1500s, a pinnacle was reached in the mid to late 1700s. Most of those that remain today come from that period.

The figures of that period most often had heads sculpted of terra cotta with inset glass eyes and intricately carved wooden hands and feet on hemp-wrapped, wire-frame bodies. Other materials such as wax, papier mache and ivory were used but not to the extent of wood and terra cotta.

Nativity scene figures were made until the late 1800s, but the quality declined, as did the interest for and the care of the figures, so not many of these are available.

The hand-carved wooden creche scene by Tita Ling of the Philippines is a modern example of the finest workmanship.

FOREIGN (NATIVE COSTUME)

Every country in the world has produced dolls for generations, for export, or as souvenir dolls. They are dressed in authentic native costumes. Almost every conceivable material has been used in making these dolls. They are usually made of materials most readily available in the country of origin. Most of the dolls pictured in this book came into this country in the 1930s, with the exception of the "Chinese Theatrical Dolls" and the "Japanese Nobility Dolls," which are earlier. The dolls of plastic are obviously from the 1950s.

FRENCH BISQUE

There is no doubt that some dolls with bisque heads were made in the 1850s, perhaps some even earlier. The earlier dolls were the shoulder head type with the head and shoulders molded together.

On May 8, 1858, a patent was granted to Miss Marie Antoinette Leontine Rohmer, manufacturer, for a new kind of head with a cord running through the head into the body. This held the head in place but also allowed it to be turned from side to side (swivel). This could be the so-called Belton or Belton Type, as dolls with this type head are often called that by today's collectors.

In the early 1860s the Jumeau firm brought out a doll with a bisque swivel head on a bisque shoulder plate. It had glass inset eyes and an elaborately styled wig of mohair or human hair. It had the demure, sophisticated expression of a lady and was far more life-like than those with molded hair. After several experimental bodies, which avid collectors seek, an all-kid body was used. As the doll represented a very fashionable lady, it was lavishly dressed in a luxurious costume reflecting the latest Paris fashions including accessories. Consequently dolls of this type are usually called French Fashion dolls.

This was the beginning of a new era in the doll industry. For the next twenty-five years the focus of the world market shifted from Germany to France. From the 1860s to the late 1890s the leading French doll manufacturers invented various improvements and were granted many patents which revolutionized the doll industry.

Some dolls representing children were made around 1875, but they were not mass produced until after 1880. The Jumeau firm introduced a little girl doll in the early 1880s. This doll was appealing and child-like with large eyes having depth and detail similar to the human eye. They are often called "paper-weight" eyes. This doll attained great popularity at once and was soon copied by Bru and other French doll manufacturers. The little girl dolls were called "bebes." The fashion dolls had been called "poupee."

Meanwhile, the doll manufacturers in Germany had rallied, and having copied the French dolls, were producing dolls of excellent quality and were selling them at a much more reasonable price than the French. Consequently, many of the major French companies were facing financial disaster. In 1899 they amalgamated to form the Society Francaise de Fabrication de Bebes et Jouets (S.F.B.J.). The S.F.B.J. firm was in operation for fifty-nine years, from 1899 to 1958. During that time they produced adorable character face dolls which are so very much in demand today. However, mold numbers 60 and 301, and some without an incised mold number, have the dolly type face. "Unice France" (1921) is a mark that was used by S.F.B.J. These dolls usually have high coloring and are rather poor bisque, but there are exceptions. Mold No. 271 is a very desirable doll with the "Unis" mark. Some other fine dolls also have this mark.

Two of the S.F.B.J. characters in this book are in the sub-category "BABIES." The "nurser" is on a toddler type body; the other one with a flange neck is on a cloth body.

Some of the famous French doll manufacturers were Bru, Gaultier, Gesland, Huret, Jumeau, Rohmer, Schmitt, and Steiner.

GERMAN BISQUE

In the 1840s through the 1870s some of the famous potteries of Copenhagen and Dresden made beautiful bisque dolls' heads of superlative quality. These are considered to be some of the most beautiful dolls ever produced. They were made of tinted and untinted bisque. Collectors often call the untinted bisque "parian" because the complexions resemble a type of marble. These dolls, with their delicate and perfect features and fashionably molded hair, are very rare and valuable today. Many of these dolls have other decorations such as a molded yoke, collar, snood, ribbons, bows, flowers, and jewelry. Dolls of this type reached the height of their popularity in the 1870s. The earlier heads had painted eyes and were the shoulder-head type. Like the china-head dolls, they are dated by the style of the molded hair, which represents the period they were produced, even though production continued for a number of years.

The period 1860 through the 1870s was a golden era in the doll industry. A swivel head had been invented and some of the dolls of this period had a wig and glass eyes. These were usually put on a young girl or lady type cloth doll. Some had kid arms while others had bisque arms and

7

legs. These dolls' heads were often the portrait type, made to resemble ladies of nobility or other famous people. The early shoulder-head dolls were unmarked. Sometime later the bisque-head doll with a mache/wood jointed adult body replaced those formerly made of cloth or kid. A later revival of the portrait type lady doll was around 1910 when the Kestner firm brought out a doll modeled to resemble the Gibson Girl. Other examples of adult type dolls are those pictured that have the mache/wood jointed bodies of the flapper era.

In the 1880 to 1900 period figurines and piano babies were very popular. They were made in Germany and France. Gebruder Heubach was noted for the quality of the bisque and the beautifully detailed molded clothes of these figures. Many had intaglio eyes for which Heubach was famous.

Naughty Nudies are a type of figurine doll introduced in the early 1900s depicting nude ladies in various poses.

Late in the nineteenth century bisque heads for dolls were made larger in proportion to the body than those previously used on the adult-type body dolls. During the 1880s they began to dress these dolls like children.

In the early 1890s the German doll manufacturers, having rebuilt their industry, began mass producing many fine dolls comparable to the quality of the French dolls.

Portrait and character type dolls became very popular around the turn of the century. Doll heads were modeled to resemble real children, and their features were modeled to portray various expressions of emotion characteristic of children of all ages. Production continued into the 1920s.

In the late 1890s baby dolls usually had the round dolly-type face and a short dumpy kid body. Around 1909 Kammer & Reinhart brought out a baby doll with a character face, mold No. 100, and a bent limb mache/wood jointed body that resembled the body of a real baby. Some of the baby dolls of this era had a similar type mache/wood jointed baby body and others had a cloth body used with the head that had a flange neck.

The much loved "Bye-Lo" baby created by Grace Storey Putnam in 1922 was one of the last bisque-head dolls produced. "My Dream Baby" was brought out in 1924 by Armand Marseille in competition with the "Bye-Lo."

Some of the leading German doll manufacturers were Heinrich Handwerck, Heubach-Koppelsdorf (Ernst Heubach), Gebruder Heubach, Kammer & Reinhart, J. D. Kestner, Jr., Armand Marseille, and Simon and Halbig.

JAPANESE BISQUE

Production of bisque-head dolls in Japan was stepped up during World War I when the manufacture of dolls came to a halt in Germany. The Japanese often copied the Germans, but they did not produce the fine quality, detail, and workmanship that was characteristic of the German dolls. Morimura Brothers and many of the large doll manufacturers in Japan were actually American companies that distributed dolls and often designed the bisque heads. By 1925 production of dolls dropped sharply in Japan, as Germany was again producing dolls for the world market. The Morimura Bros. mark is incised on many of these bisque-head dolls and some are marked "Nippon."

MECHANICAL

Mechanical dolls and toys have always been most fascinating to children and adults alike. Most mechanicals had music boxes or some noise maker as well as the action mechanism. The French, especially the Jumeau company, mechanized their exquisite dolls to make some of the most beautiful mechanicals of the 1870s and 1880s.

The dolls pushing carts in this Price Guide are similar to those patented by Charles Hawkins September 8, 1868, and William Goodwin of the same year.

Marotts, Folly Heads or "dolls on sticks," with music boxes or squeakers under their costumes, were most popular in the 1890s. Both French and German companies produced them.

METAL

Metal heads for dolls were made as early as 1861. Many metal dolls' heads and small all-metal dolls were on the market about 1899. Although Alfred Vischer and Company had used the name "Minerva" on their metal head dolls since 1894, this trademark was not patented in the U. S. until 1901.

Some of the best metal dolls' heads marked "Diana" were made by Alfred Heller of Germany. He registered this trademark in the U. S. in 1903.

Karl Standfuss made dolls with metal heads marked "Juno," which were distributed in the U. S. by Borgfeldt about this same time.

MISCELLANEOUS MATERIALS

Several ages and materials of dolls are placed in this category. There is virtually no material known that hasn't been used in making dolls.

Darrow's rawhide dolls were patented May 1, 1866, and production continued into the 1870s.

Moroccan leather (goatskin) dolls from Tangiers, Africa, were made for a few years in the late 1940s.

Seminole Indian dolls, made from cypress fiber, were sold for many years as souvenirs by the Florida Indians. These date in the 1940s.

The Shirley Temple soap doll is from the late 1930s.

Cornshucks, nuts and other materials have been made into dolls by country craftsmen for many generations.

Eskimos have always carved ivory dolls and animal toys from walrus tusks for their children. The doll "with it's skin outfit" pictured in this book is from the early 1900s.

Walt Disney items have been produced in various materials. The porcelain "Mickey Mouse" is just one example of these characters of the late 1930s.

PAPIER MACHE

Papier mache is said to have been used for dolls heads as early as the 1500s. The German,

so-called "Milliners' Models," are among the earliest types of dolls to be mass produced. Their mache heads have hair styles from 1810 to the 1850s and were produced in great numbers, with little change, for at least that many years. Their bodies are hand-sewn kid leather with wooden arms and legs.

Ludwig Greiner of Philadelphia was probably making mache doll heads in the 1840s. He is credited with the "Pre-Greiner" types with pupil-less eyes. He obtained the earliest U. S. doll head patent, March 30, 1858, and extended this patent in 1872. Production was continued to 1900 by his sons.

Other maches of this type (M & S Superior, Unbreakable Heads, Cuno & Otto Dressel, Gold Medal, etc.), nearly all were made in the 1870s and the 1880s.

PLASTIC AND VINYL

The modern history of plastics began about 1860. Since that time plastic materials in various formulas have been introduced in the United States. Vinyl, introduced in 1951, is simply one of a number of different plastic materials. It is very durable and its soft mat finish on the modern dolls make them quite life-like.

Many of the companies that made composition dolls in the 1920s to 1940s continued in operation and produced dolls of plastic in the late 1940s and the 1950s. Vinyl was used extensively in the 1950s and 1960s in the doll industry, and is a primary material of the 1970s. There are several books on these modern collectible dolls currently on the market, so we will note only a few of them here, although some are no longer available in toy shops and stores.

Madame Alexander Doll Company has produced many dolls especially popular with children. "Alice" of *Alice in Wonderland* began a trend that continues with Louisa May Alcott's *Little Women*, characters from the movie *Sound of Music*, and James W. Riley's *Little Orphan Annie*. Some of their other modern creations are The Madam Doll, the International Dolls, the Portrettes, and the Portrait Children.

American Character Doll Company made the Betsy McCall doll in 1961 in hard plastic, and

Tiny Tears in hard plastic combined with other materials in the 1950s and the 1960s, and the all-vinyl dolls in the mid 1960s.

Effenbee made the hard plastic Honey Walker in the 1950s and continues to produce adorable all-vinyl baby dolls.

Ideal Toy Corporation made the hard plastic Saucy Walker doll in the 1950s and the vinyl Kissy around 1961, as well as many others.

The original Terri Lee dolls date from 1948. Jerri Lee dolls were introduced later the same year. Tiny Terri, Linda Lee and Baby Linda came out in 1951, Connie Lynn in 1955, and So Sleepy in 1957. Terri Lee had an extensive wardrobe and was said to be one of the best dressed dolls in the world. The Talking Terri Lee which came with a record was called "The National Baby Sitter."

RUBBER

It was not until Charles Goodyear discovered the vulcanizing process for soft rubber in the late 1840s that dolls and dolls' heads were made of rubber in any number. Charles' and Nelson's (his brother) processes and patents were used by several manufacturers in the 1850s to 1870s. Many of these are marked with the Goodyear patent date, May 6, 1851. The use of rubber continued but in smaller volume, and more for small all-rubber dolls, until the advent of vinyl after World War II.

The Dye Dee Baby, the So-Wee, and the Tiny Tears dolls of the 1940s and 1950s are notable as examples of the late use of rubber for dolls.

The Walt Disney "Dopey" made by Seiberling Latex is another example of the various materials that were used to make these characters. The one pictured in this book is from the 1940s to 1950s.

WAX

Wax has been used for making dolls since ancient times in Italy and Greece and somewhat later in England, France, and Germany. A study of types gives a general guide to dating. Whether made of all-wax-over-papier-mache, few of these dolls are marked. Therefore they are difficult to date.

Most of the wax dolls of the early 1800s were of the poured type, often reinforced on the inside by plaster of paris. A few of the wax-over-mache dolls with slit heads date in the 1840s, but most are later. The mid 1800s marked a zenith in poured wax doll production with those made in England by the Montanaris, the Pierottis, and a few other companies.

The greatest volume of wax dolls are wax-over-papier-mache and the later wax-over-composition produced from the 1860s into the 1880s. The painting of the earlier type was done on the mache and waxed-over, whereas the later ones were painted on the wax coat itself. One other dating hint is that most of those before 1860 had flat soled shoes or feet (usually wood) that often came beautifully molded and/or painted.

Production declined in the 1890s and was nearly non-existent after 1900, except in England.

Five generations of the Vargas family in New Orleans have produced wax character figures. Those pictured in this book are from the early 1900s.

WOOD

Wood has been used for making dolls since early recorded time. A few examples of seventeenth and eighteenth century English wooden dolls, the so called "Queen Ann" dolls, are in existence today.

German peg wooden dolls were produced in great numbers in the early 1800s. These are also called Dutch dolls. They are the type collected by Queen Victoria. The later German-Dutch dolls had fewer joints and were much cruder, but they continued into the early 1900s.

Joel Ellis of Springfield, Vermont, produced America's first commercial wooden doll in the early 1870s. He patented the doll in 1873 but ceased production a year later. Other dolls of this type were made by Mason and Taylor and Charles Johnson through the 1880s.

Albert Schoenhut, a toy maker in Philadelphia, brought out his dolls in 1909. These first dolls had character faces. They were patented January 17, 1911. Dolly face dolls with painted eyes appeared in 1915. Decal eyes were used in 1920 and sleep eyes in 1921. By 1924 the metal spring joints were replaced by elastic cord.

DOLL PRICES — WHAT DETERMINES THEM?

The dolls shown in this WALLACE-HOMESTEAD PRICE GUIDE TO DOLLS are dolls in fine-to-excellent condition and are priced accordingly. As there are many factors in determining the value of a doll, let's look at the most important ones.

Condition: Because you expect an old doll to show minor wear—nose rubs where it's been kissed time and again; scuffed toes, slightly chipped fingers; because the doll may show a factory defect—none of these reasons should detract from the doll's value. That perfect in-the-original-box, never-used doll—everyone's dream (and, possibly a reproduction) may turn up once in awhile, but don't pay top dollar for a doll that needs a new wig, restringing, eyes reset, or new clothes. Added up, these expenses mean you're paying more than the doll's worth, unless, of course, it's rare.

Clothing: The most desirable, naturally, are the original clothes in good-to-excellent condition. If the clothing has been replaced, it should reflect the style and fashion when the doll was made. Lots of collectors dress their own dolls. You should, however, save the original clothing whenever possible.

Marks: Obviously, a marked doll is worth more than one unmarked, all things being equal. Most dolls are marked on the back of the head in the shoulder area; some are marked on the body. It takes a while to know where to look but it's worth it when you find a collector's item.

Complete Originality: Here again, if everything—head, body, wig, clothing, hands, feet—is original, it's worth a good deal more than a "married" doll, one that has been assembled from two or three different dolls. But, a completely original doll of any age is fast becoming a thing of the past. Don't turn your nose up at a good buy simply because the wig's not original, etc.

Quality: Just that. One doll is professionally made, decorated, dressed. The other? Quantity. Obviously, select the **quality** doll. Look for human-looking faces, eyes. Bisque heads can have that warm look; on the other hand, cheaply decorated bisque heads look harsh. Avoid them.

Size: Generally, a small doll brings a small price; just the opposite for a large doll. The exception is the very large or the very small doll. But then, if you like it, buy it!

Age: The older, rare types command high prices. But, age is not the determining factor in most cases. Is the doll readily available? Is it rare? One of a kind? Some of the twentieth century dolls bring a higher price than the older, more rare types. It's just one more thing to keep in mind when buying a doll.

Body: Equally as important as the doll's head. Skillfully repaired bodies are acceptable; the wrong body drastically lowers the value of any two-part doll. Vinyl dolls with stained bodies should be avoided as well as cracked and/or peeling all-compo dolls. If you possess common sense, use it.

In closing, *Caveat Emptor.* "Let the buyer beware!" There are skilled reproductions making the rounds at the shops and at the antiques shows, not to mention a lot of auctions. The French Fashions, China Heads and Frozen Charlies seem to be the most prevalent, **but** there are others. So, be careful, because a reproduction doll dressed in old clothing can (and will) fool a lot of nice people. Just because the doll is unwrapped from a 1900s newspaper doesn't mean it's that old.

Hopefully, we've given you some information that will come in handy when you buy a doll. Experience is a great teacher, so study everything you can get your hands on. Just keep in mind that a lot of factors are involved here and you're not going to learn everything overnight. The fact that you've purchased this WALLACE-HOMESTEAD PRICE GUIDE TO DOLLS shows you've got a lot of common sense. Tell your friends!

GLOSSARY OF DOLL TERMS

— A —

age of dolls: Advertisements, catalogs, illustrations—all are helpful in determining the age of the doll. So also are trademarks, patents, copyrights, hair styles, and shoe styles. Keep in mind that the doll may have a head and body that were made by different firms.

all-bisque dolls: Most have shoulder joints; few are fully jointed. Generally, they're small dolls and were quite popular in the 1880s and especially collectible during the Kewpie era in the twentieth century.

aluminum: A silvery, lightweight, easily-worked metal that was used for dolls at the end of the nineteenth century until the early 1920s.

all steel dolls: With fully ball-jointed limbs, the entire doll was made of thin sheet steel; handpainted, jointed at ankles and wrists, strung with steel springs. They were invented in 1902-03 by Vincent Lake.

American dolls: Until after the Civil War (or the War Between the States), few dolls were produced commercially. During the latter part of the nineteenth century, New York, New England, and Philadelphia became principal doll making centers. During World War I, American made dolls were in high demand, and New York City and its neighbor across the Hudson, New Jersey, became internationally known for their doll making.

art dolls: Created by skilled craftsmen, these dolls were inspired by stage and screen personalities, famous works of art, etc. Rose O'Neill of Kewpie doll fame was one of the many artists. One wonders if the dolls inspired by Donatello's babies had any connection with the Donatello line produced by the Roseville Pottery Company in 1915.

Austrian dolls: Before World War I, many hand carved wooden dolls were made in Austria. Around 1800 a delicate china baby doll was made in Vienna. Leo Katz, Franz Frankl, and Heinrich Dehler were just a few Austrians who made fine dolls.

— B —

baby bodies: Until the beginning of the nineteenth century, the word "baby" encompassed dolls of all ages; in the eighteenth and early nineteenth centuries, wax and wooden dools were dressed as babies, had very short arms, and were chubbier than the larger dolls.

baby dolls: At the turn of the twentieth century, dolls with the proportions of a baby came into vogue, lips slightly parted to take the nipple of a bottle, chubbier bodies with shorter limbs.

bald heads: Early twentieth century "baldheads" referred to dolls with painted and molded hair. In the nineteenth century, this term seemingly referred to dolls' heads whose crowns were not cut off. This type of doll is found in all kinds of material, bald, china-heads with wigs—as late as the beginning of the twentieth century and possibly later.

ball joints: A ball (usually wood) and two adjacent sockets strung with elastic or some other material to permit the joint to move in any direction.

bent limb: Baby bodies that did not use ball joints. Invented in Germany in 1909.

bebe: The French word for baby.

bebe incassable: Translated from the French, "unbreakable baby." The French applied this term when describing their bisque-head, jointed, composition-bodied dolls. The term first appeared in advertisements in the 1870s.

"Belton-type" dolls: Dolls with bald heads made of bisque.

"Biedermeier" china-head doll: A bald, china-head to which a wig was attached. Some refer to the "Biedermeier" period as those years between 1815 and 1850. Others say china-heads of this style were probably made after 1850. Bald china-head doll advertisements appeared in catalogs as late as 1915.

bisque: In ceramics this describes pottery and other earthenware finished in one firing and not intended to be glazed. Some bisque-head dolls do have heads that have glossy parts as decoration.

bonnet dolls: Sometimes wax but usually bisque-head dolls with molded bonnets (hats).

boxwood: Some Parisian dolls were made of this material in the early 1900s.

breadcrumbs: Another material used in making dolls.

breast plate dolls' heads: An American term denoting a doll's head with shoulders attached.

bust heads: A term usually associated with the French, denoting a doll's head with shoulders attached.

Buster Brown: Originally, a cartoon strip created by Richard F. Outcault in 1902 that appeared in the old *New York Herald.* Buster and his dog Tige appeared as dolls in 1904.

butterfly doll: A bonnet-type doll with molded butterfly headdress. About 1901.

Bye-Lo Baby: A "life-sized" baby (three days old) doll designed and copyrighted by Grace Storey Putnam in 1922, the first of four such copyrights.

— C —

Canadian dolls: Dolls manufactured in Canada after the outbreak of World War I until around 1925. The industry boomed at first, then slowly was confronted with many difficulties—procurement of eyes, clothing, shoes, etc. It eventually was discontinued.

celluloid dolls: These dolls were made by the Hyatt brothers (John W. and Isaiah S.) in the 1860s—some say as early as 1863, though the trade name "celluloid" was not used until 1869 or thereabouts. A synthetic material discovered in England basically composed of pyroxylin and camphor.

character dolls: After 1900, a doll that was made to look like a real person, such as Shirley Temple, Charlie Chaplin, etc. Usually bisque or composition.

china-head dolls: Made of white clay, tinted, fired, dipped in glaze and refired. Appearing on the market as early as the 1750s, they didn't achieve their zenith of popularity until the 1840s. Pressed china-heads usually preceded the poured ones, manufacture-wise.

china-limb dolls: In the 1840s and 1850s, these dolls had jointed wooden bodies. Later, other materials such as cloth were used. Cloth bodies had no joints or were made sometimes with swinging-type joints. The legs had molded-and-painted shoes and stockings. Later the shoes were made with heels, and garters were painted on the stockings.

clay dolls: Material from the river banks was used in medieval times, probably even earlier, to make crude dolls.

cloverleaf dolls: Bonnet-type doll with molded headdress in shape of cloverleaf, porcelain limbs, pink muslin body. From about the turn of the century.

composition dolls: A wood pulp mixture is used to make this type of doll. Some had wigs, some had painted hair.

cork pates: France, nineteenth and twentieth century; used on dolls' heads.

corozo: Dolls made in Ecuador were composed of a vegetable ivory type of material. This same material is being used in China (both Republic and People's Republic) today to make "ivory" items such as statuettes, cigarette boxes, etc.

— D —

doll: A children's toy made to resemble a baby, child or grown person. English dictionaries used the word as early as 1700, but the word wasn't used commonly in America until around 1745-50.

Dresden: Certain glazed china-heads with the crossed-sword mark of the Dresden factory at Meissen, Germany. Johann Bottger developed the first quality porcelain in the early 1700s. Most Dresden in the U. S. was brought in by importers in the late nineteenth century.

dried apple dolls: Made by the people in the Appalachian region of North Carolina in the 1920s. The original dolls represented the sang root diggers. These dolls were also made in the northwest in the 1910s, depicting Indians.

— E —

enamel bisque: A type of unbreakable composition used in the 1920s.

enamel eyes: Fine eyes with parts of glass fastened together.

eye color: The early wooden and wax dolls (late eighteenth century) usually had dark brown or black eyes. Brown eyes are fairly scarce on china-head dolls; violet eyes are very, very rare. The many shades of blue eyes can possibly be attributed to the different formulas that made up the glass batch.

— F —

fabric dolls: Just that —made of cloth or felt. Some dolls were made from cotton sheets by a manufacturer to advertise his product—usually sheets and towels.

faces: The shape of the doll's face generally indicates the age of the person it represents. Doll's faces vary because each was painted by hand. Good artists painted good faces; great artists painted great faces.

fashion dolls: The word "fashion" is almost synonymous with the French dolls of the late 1800s. The Jumeaus revolutionized the doll industry in the 1860s, producing a doll with a bisque head, life-like face, set-in eyes and elaborately-made wig, not to mention fabulous clothes. These were so perfect, minutely so, that the dolls made by the Jumeaus became known as "French Fashion" dolls even though most collectors agree that Jumeaus' dolls were made for the children and were not intended for the fashion industry.

feet: Dolls' feet were made of china, wood, kid, poured wax, cloth, leather, aluminum, composition, rag, bisque.

five-in-one-doll: Five screw-on heads distinguished this particular doll made of celluloid around 1912. One of the five heads was that of a cat!

Flanders babies: An early name for dolls with wooden bodies.

flange necks: A design where the cloth is sewn over the flange, holding the head to the body but permitting the head to rotate from side to side. Usually found on composition, bisque, or china-head dolls used with cloth bodies, 1860s on.

"Flirting-Eye" dolls: The eyes move from side to side, not up and down. Usually papier-mache or bisque. Known in the trade as Goo-Goo eyes. Eddie Cantor used them for years!

flock: Fibers glued or pasted onto a doll for decoration, usually made of hair or cloth—used for short, boy's type hair. As early as 1850s.

folly heads: A whirling musical doll, complete with bells, that played a tune when whirled around. Usually with bisque head, late 1800s to early 1920s. Also call "marotte."

French bisque: A blonde bisque head, generally associated with France, but also made in Germany.

French dolls: "Bebe, you've come a long, long way!" Empires fell, wars were fought and the competition was severe, but, through it all, from the seventeenth century on, the French dolls were among the most beautiful and artistic ever made anywhere. Then, in the early years of the 1900s, the German doll makers cut into the French doll market. But, in the minds and hearts of so many, many doll collectors, there just isn't any doll that can compare to a French doll!

frozen Charlottes: "Solid china," "pillar dolls," "bathing beauties"—call them what you will. They come in both glazed and unglazed porcelain. Some were so small they were used as favors in cakes. They came with wigs, bonnets, molded hair, in black, white, pink china. From the 1850s on.

— G —

German dolls: For centuries fine dolls came from Germany. Cheap labor, schools to teach how to make dolls, readily available raw material—all these contributed to making dolls from Germany some of the finest the world has ever seen.

German bisque: As with French bisque, not all German bisque was made in Germany. The heads were highly colored.

glue: Used as the adhesive agent in the manufacture of papier-mache and composition dolls. Those made before World War I, using glue and flour with a "cold" press, tended to peel and were often affected by temperature change.

Godey-head: A blonde or brunette china-head doll, with molded headdress of vertical pointed curls.

Goo-Goo dolls: A trade name, virtually the same as "Flirting-Eye" dolls. Usually they came with real eyelashes.

Greiner dolls: Greiner (Ludwig) made papier-mache dolls' heads; he took out the first U.S. patent for a doll's head in 1858.

gutta-percha: A rubber-like substance in its raw state, reddish white in color, workable by hot water alone, retaining its shape when cooled. Popular as a doll substance in the 1850s. Unlike rubber, it will not float.

— H —

hands: Basically the same material was used here that was used for feet.

"Hottentots": All-celluloid Negro Kewpies; they came as a pair in a blue/white blanket, wings painted white, 3¼" high.

— I —

intaglio eyes: Painted eyes with the iris and pupil concave.

ivory porcelain: Another name for china used to make doll's heads.

— J —

Johnny doll: These were English sailor dolls, made for baby boys in 1890s.

Jolly Jack: A character doll—baby boy with composition head, molded hair, stuffed body, dressed in rompers. 1912-14.

— K —

KKK: Not what you think it stands for! Simply a trademark registered by Parsons-Jackson in U.S., probably for a specific type of doll.

Kewpie: Mentioned here because it's one of the most widely-known dolls in the world. Rose O'Neill (Mrs. Wilson) designed it and received a patent for the doll in 1913. Most collectors associate the Kewpie doll with bisque but this doll was made from just about every type of material. The earlier ones were bisque or celluloid.

kid bodies: Popular during the nineteenth and early twentieth centuries. Early dolls usually had unjointed kid bodies with wooden limbs, although as early as 1842 kid bodies were made jointed.

kiss baby: A doll, jointed composition body, whose right arm bends to the doll's mouth, then throws a kiss.

knitted dolls: It's fair to assume that any woman who could make "homespun" cloth could knit a doll, no matter how crude, for her children.

— L —

large dolls: Those dolls 36'' or more in size that were made for carnivals, premiums, or displays.

London Doll Market: Before World War I agents selling for doll factories in Germany made this the largest doll market in the world. Later in the 1920s, the market shifted to New York City.

Louvre: In the first part of the twentieth century this was a large department store in Paris that sold dolls. It was not connected with the famous Paris museum of the same name.

— M —

Magyar Asszonyok x Nemzeti Szovetsege: This was the National League of Hungarian Women in Budapest. They made dolls in Hungarian costumes, 1909-25. And a happy supercalifragilistic-expialidocious to you!

mama dolls: Dolls that say "Mama!" Supposedly, they go back several centuries.

marks: These are usually found on the back of the doll's head or shoulders; sometimes found inside the head or on the soles of the feet. In rare cases, they are on the eyeball, upper arm or upper leg, or on the pate. These marks may be pressed, incised, printed, painted, embroidered, or merely attached to the doll with a ribbon, tag, or sticker.

mask face dolls: The back half of the doll's head is usually made of cloth or a material different from the stiffer or more rigid part of the face. Many celluloid dolls had this type of face.

Meissen: In the early 1700s, Johann Bottger invented the first porcelain that was considered quality. His factory was at the Royal Saxon Porcelain Works at Meissen, Saxony. His work was finely decorated and in exquisite shapes, often with raised enamel flowers. The famous crossed swords in blue are known throughout the world.

metal dolls: The French and American dollmakers made most of these just prior to the Civil War until the early 1920s.

metal heads: These were made before the entire metal doll, probably as early as 1860. The U.S. and France made some but most were made in Germany.

Mickey: This doll had nothing to do with Walt Disney. It was a hand-painted rag doll filled with sanitary floss and made around 1920 by Bandeau Sales Company.

milliners' model dolls: Supposedly, early nineteenth century dolls, with papier-mache heads and unjointed kid bodies. They were used to show new fashions before the printing of fashion magazines.

Montanari dolls: A wax doll made in England around 1850. Each hair was individually inserted in the head, eyelash into eyelid. Costumed, it was considered a doll for the wealthy.

mouths: Closed-mouth dolls made from the late 1800s on bring higher prices today because they're harder to find than the open-mouth dolls. Some varieties of dolls made around 1850 had open mouths. They were composition, wax-over-papier-mache. Later, ceramic dolls had open mouths. By 1895 many dolls were being made with an opening into the head, with parted lips and teeth showing.

multi-face dolls: Just after the Civil War a U.S. patent for a four-faced doll was obtained, the head rotating horizontally. About the same time French doll makers obtained patents for two-faced dolls. They were followed by the Germans. Some faces lifted off; other dolls had changeable heads.

multi-head dolls: At least fifteen years before the Civil War, dolls were made with two heads. One head could be removed and be replaced with another while one of the two heads was concealed by clothing. In 1920 a doll with five faces was patented and manufactured by the Moo-V-Doll Manufacturing Company, obviously aiming their product at the movie star fans.

— N —

names: As with pattern glass, giving names to dolls that originally had no name has caused a good bit of confusion. Usually, but not always, porcelain dolls had their names marked on them; or, they had tags and/or labels which were easily lost. Because the word "doll" is fairly new—years before they were called "fashion babies," "babies," "little ladies," etc.—it's difficult today to positively identify a specific doll. Collectors give a name to a doll; a name gets into print, then others call their doll by this name. Confusion and more confusion!

nature arms and legs: Simply, bent limbs on infant type dolls. They were made about 1913.

nature shaped: In the mid-1920s, this was a doll with a composition body with a molded kneecap on the lower leg and the joint above the knee—so the doll could wear the latest fashion, short dresses!

needle molding: The process of molding a cloth doll's features into three-dimensional form by stitching with a needle.

nostrils: "Made in Japan" dolls usually have pierced nostrils. Usually, two red dots indicated the nostril. These dots were often omitted on the early china-heads and papier-maches and the compos after World War I.

nude dolls: "Streakers" take note: these were simply undressed dolls that usually wore a chemise.

numbers: Some represent the size, others the mold. Numbers may also represent patent, dates, etc. Get a book and read—it can get confusing!

nuts: In Haiti, the natives have carved dolls' faces from unopened cashew nuts for more than 200 years. Until the cashew nut is shucked and roasted, its outer shell is deadly poisonous. The Haitians used sisal for hats, whiskers, other decorations. The mountain people in the southern Appalachia region have long used walnuts, hazelnuts, and the like, to carve crude faces for doll bodies. The body usually consisted of homespun stuffed with grass or straw.

— O —

Old Glory: Mentioned here because it has nothing to do with our flag. It was a trademark registered in Germany around 1905 for jointed dolls. In 1916 dolls called "Old Glory Kids," dressed in red, white, and blue, were made by the Ideal Novelty & Toy Company.

original condition: As with antique furniture, this term denotes dolls with all original parts. Even if the body is faded, and a few hairs are missing from the wig, if all the original parts are there, it can be designated as being in "original condition." The biggest mistake the beginning collector of dolls makes is to replace worn and/or cracked heads, feet, hands, etc. This is comparable to polishing a coin, cutting a stamp from an envelope or rebluing an old gun. In the early 1900s few collectors concerned themselves with the original body or original clothes. As most dolls have passed through the hands of collectors, relatives, or dealers, it's extremely difficult, if not impossible, to ascertain whether or not the doll is in "original condition" and is wearing its original costume. If in doubt, leave it alone!

Ozocerite: A substitute for beeswax, it was made from a residue of petroleum, late 1800s until mid-1920s.

— P —

paints: Remember when the government banned the use of lead-based paint for use on baby's crib? Just a few years ago! Before the eighteenth century, dolls were colored with bismuth paints which were deadly poisonous. In the early nineteenth century, white lead paint was used, also poisonous. By 1905 these paints were prohibited by law and the use of zinc oxide, or other "safe" colors, came into being. About time!

Paladin Baby: Remember "Have gun, will travel!" with Richard Boone? This "baby" doll was made in 1903 in Germany, fourteen years before Mr. Boone first saw the "light of day!"

Pandora: Depending on their size, they were either "great" or "small" Pandoras. One wonders if she carried a box, given to her by Zeus.

paperweight eyes: Some collectors use this term to denote blown glass eyes that have the quality found in fine paperweights, depth and detail.

Parian: A semi-vitreous paste porcelain resembling Carrara marble, it was first made by Copeland in England in 1842. Obviously, it was used to make dolls' heads in the bisque form.

pate: The hole found in the top of many dolls' heads. Generally, the wig is attached to the pate. Pates are made from cardboard, composition, cork, etc.

peddler dolls: Carved from wood and carrying a basket filled with miniature articles.

pointed torso: At one time a great number of dolls were made with the bottom of their torso ending in a point. A hole, going through from side to side, was for attaching the legs.

portrait dolls: Dolls that portrayed real people have been around for a long time. Queen Victoria was a favorite subject, as was Jenny Lind. A great many stage and screen stars have been used as models. Some were good, some were awful!

pottery dolls: These were made in Europe and in the U.S. during the nineteenth century. Rookwood Pottery in Cincinnati, Ohio, made a few dolls' heads, around 1912 to 1920. These heads are rare and expensive when found intact.

Poupards: Simply dolls without legs; babies wrapped in long, thin bands of cloth (swaddling).

pre-Greiner dolls: German, 1830s to 1850s, papier-mache heads, blown glass eyes, quite large.

pyralin: Apparently DuPont made this product in the 1920s with doll manufacturers in mind. A plastic-like material.

— Q —

— R —

rag dolls: The ancient Greeks, Romans, and Egyptians made rag dolls for their children. The pioneer women of America made dolls from homespun cloth. When father's socks wore out, mother stuffed same with grass or hay and daughter had a doll, after father painted on a face or mother used buttons for the eyes and mouth.

Rembrandt hair: Late 1800s until after World War I, there was a style of hairdo where the hair was cut in bangs across the forehead, fell straight around the sides and the back of the head. Sounds like a modern-day haircut, doesn't it?

roguish eyes: Goo-Goo eyes.

rubber dolls: Crude rubber dolls go back several centuries. When Goodyear discovered vulcanizing, a method that made rubber hold its shape, rubber then became an important substance from which to make dolls.

16

— S —

sawdust: Used to stuff dolls along with other materials such as cotton, cork or hair. Sawdust was also used as one of the ingredients for making certain composition bodies and heads.

skittle dolls: Turned wooden dolls shaped like skittles (ninepins); made in Sonneberg, Thur., and elsewhere, 1730s to mid-1920s.

sleeping eyes: As early as the 1700s, dolls had eyes that opened and closed. Counterweight eyes seem to have come into use in the early 1800s, becoming popular at the end of the century.

Sonneberg, Thur.: Believe it or not, in the early 1900s a Sonneberg factory turned out over 2,000,000 dolls of one variety. The china factories were capable of producing more than 20,000,000 dolls' heads a year. Small wonder that it was known as the doll center of the world. As with Henry Ford's assembly line for the Model T, so at Sonneberg each worker had a specific task. One would paint eyes, one would paint lips, etc.

Springfield dolls: Wooden dolls made by Joel Ellis in Springfield, Vermont, from early 1870s until about 1885. Mason & Taylor also made the same type of doll, same town, same years. The Ellis doll is rare and highly collectible.

starfish hands: Doll hands with the fingers spread apart like a starfish. After 1910.

stiff-jointed dolls: Doll limbs that moved only in a backward and forward direction.

stoneware: Doll heads were made of this material. Though it's usually associated with a crude earthenware, some items were made of salt-glazed ware, basalt, and other formulations. It is doubtful if the latter materials were ever used for making doll heads. There is no evidence to show that dolls' heads were ever made by Weller or Roseville, two potteries that operated in the Zanesville, Ohio, area, in the late 1800s.

— T —

talking dolls: As mentioned previously, bellows and pipe reeds were used to make the dolls "talk." Thomas Edison invented and manufactured phonograph dolls as early as 1875-6. During 1878-79, he had thirteen different patents to protect his discovery.

Tommy Atkins: A doll made in the early 1900s, the name taken from a poem by Rudyard Kipling.

topsy turvy dolls: A head at either end of the doll, one hidden in the skirt while the other showed. Various materials were used to make the heads, rag, composition, etc.

— V —

Vanity Fair dolls: China-head dolls (limbs also of china) on a muslin body. A molded gilt necklace with an oval mirror as a pendant, was part of the shoulder head. Early 1900s.

Vera dolls: A type of doll offered as a subscription premium, in this case, *Youth's Companion*, late 1890s.

Virginia Dare: A baby doll made by Averill Mfg. Co. around 1917. Virginia Dare was the name given to the first child born at Jamestown, Virginia, in 1609. Her parents' marriage was "the first recorded English marriage on the soil of the United States."

— W —

walking dolls: First made in Germany in the seventeenth century; in Paris in the 1730s. Most nineteenth century "walking dolls" had a clockwork device to propel them.

wax dolls: These go back to the early Romans. In Bavaria they were made from the seventeenth century on, in England from mid-1700s on, in France in the eighteenth century. In the mid-nineteenth century, expensive wax dolls were made by the Montanaris, the Pierottis, and others. In the early 1900s a lot of confusion as to what was and what was not a wax doll was caused by collectors who wrongly called bisque dolls wax dolls.

wire-eyed dolls: These were wax dolls with sleeping eyes. A wire at the waist made the eyes open and close, apparently a substitute for counterweights.

wooden dolls: They go back to the days of the early Egyptians. Anyone who could whittle made dolls from wood. As early as the mid-1500s, wooden dolls were known in England. The Austrians and Bavarians were experts in this field as early as the seventeenth century.

— X —

— Y —

Yellow Kid doll: Five years before he created the Buster Brown comic strip, Dick Outcault created this cartoon character, the first to use colored comic sheets, in 1895. The doll first appeared in 1897. It was of composition, jointed, attired in yellow tissue paper.

— Z —

Obviously, there are many, many terms dealing with dolls not mentioned in this Glossary. If we've helped you in any way, it has been worth the effort. Look for more doll terms in our next edition.

SELECTED
DOLLS
IN COLOR

ARMAND MARSEILLE DREAM BABY, bisque flange head marked A M GER-
MANY 341/0; painted hair, glass sleep eyes, closed mouth, cloth body, celluloid hands.
10″ long, head circumference 9″. **$175-225.**

COMPANY UNIDENTIFIED, bisque shoulder
head, slightly turned, marked GERMANY 2759/0,
mohair wig, sleep eyes, eyelashes, open mouth, kid
body and legs, bisque forearms. 15″ tall. **$150-175.**

CELLULOID BABY, socket head marked FRANCE Eagle
Head 30; molded/painted hair, sleep eyes with lashes, closed
mouth, spring strung. 11½″ tall. **$200-225.**

18

STEIFF ANIMALS with metal Steiff button on each. Goose, 8″ tall $70-80. Mouse, 4″ tall $50-60. Rabbit, 8½″ long $70-80.

MAROTTE (doll on a stick), bisque flange head, marked 3200 AM 10/0 x DEP; mohair wig, inset glass eyes, open mouth, music box plays when doll is twirled on stick. 14″ tall (doll 6″, stick 8″). All original. $350-375.

KAMMER & REINHARDT, bisque socket head marked K star R SIMON & HALBIG 117 n, Germany 62; human hair wig, glass flirty sleep eyes that can stay open when lying down (naughty baby) or close (good baby); open mouth, mache/wood jointed body. 25″ tall. $750-850.

J.D.K., bisque socket head, marked MADE IN GERMANY J.D.K. 257 31; human hair wig, sleep eyes with lashes, open mouth, two teeth, quiver tongue, composition baby body. 13″ tall. $325-375. (In baby's lap) STEIFF TEDDY BEAR with original "Original Teddy" tag. $70-80.

HUMMEL DOLLS, all rubber, swivel head, molded/painted hair, painted features. Marked head and body M.I. HUMMEL, © W. GOEBEL, bee mark. Girl 11½" tall, boy 12" tall. $120-140 each.

KLEY & HAHN, bisque socket head, marked 250 K H WAULKURE 2¹/₈ GERMANY; human hair wig, open mouth, sleep eyes, composition/wood body. 22" tall. $250-300.

HEUBACH, marked MADE IN GERMANY, sunburst mark; all bisque, molded/painted hair, features, and clothes; intaglio eyes. 13" tall. $500-550 each.

20

C.M. BERGMANN—SIMON & HALBIG, bisque socket head marked C.M. BERGMANN—SIMON & HALBIG 8½, tiny red 18 on forehead; human hair wig, sleep eyes, open mouth, wood and composition body. 21" tall. $275-300.

PERUVIAN man and woman, composition heads, molded/painted hair and features, cloth bodies, jointed at shoulders and hips. 11″ tall. **$90-100 each**.

REVALO, bisque socket head marked REVALO DEP; molded hair with pink ribbon band, closed mouth with molded teeth, intaglio eyes, cloth-covered composition body, all original. 13″ tall. **$900-1,000**.

S.F.B.J. bisque socket head, marked S.F.B.J. Paris 9, incised; human hair wig, open mouth, inset eyes, mache/wood jointed body. Body marked FABRICATION FRANCAISE S.F.B.J. PARIS. 23″ tall. **$600-650**.

KAMMER & REINHARDT "Character," bisque socket head marked K star R SIMON & HALBIG 128 62; mohair wig, sleep eyes, open mouth, tremble tongue, mache baby body. 26″ tall, head circumference 16¼″. **$650-700**.

PINOCCHIO, composition swivel head, molded/painted hair and features, wood jointed body, painted clothes. Marked DES. and © by Walt Disney, made by IDEAL NOVELTY & TOY CO. 11″ tall. **$100-125.**

MECHANICAL JUMEAU, bisque socket head, paperweight eyes, pierced ears, closed mouth, human hair wig. Head nods side-to-side, hand moves up and down, body turns, foot kicks back and forth as music box plays. 20″ tall. **$3,000-3,330.**

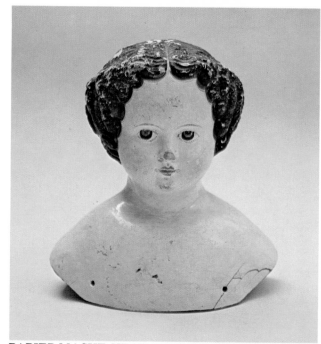

22

PAPIER-MACHE HEAD, no marks, painted brown eyes. 10″ tall, 9″ across shoulders, head circumference 18½″. **$200-225.**

DOLL DRESSMAKER'S MANNEQUIN, early eighteenth century, Flemish. Head, torso, arms, and hands carved, painted wood; head, shoulders, and hands coated with gesso and painted, glass eyes. Bottom part of mannequin is a wooden stand. 25″ tall. Too rare to compute reliable range.

CRECHE DOLL, carved wood coated with gesso and painted; glass inset eyes, open/closed mouth with teeth. 25″ tall. $1,000-1,050.

HALF DOLL ON BRUSH, marked Made in Germany 74503; molded/painted hair and shawl, white luster hat and fringe. 8″ overall. $175-200.

23

BERLINER DOLLS made in Berlin in 1972. Padded wire armature for body; face is stockinette over foam. Elf, 12″ tall. $50-60. The Knitter, 13″ tall. $50-60.

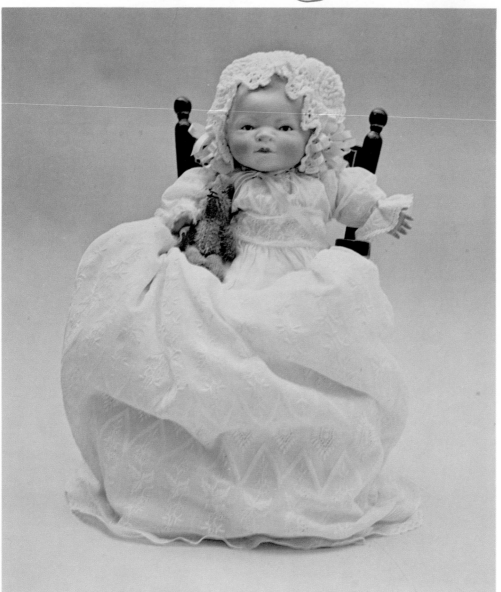

BYE-LO, bisque swivel head marked Copr. BY GRACE S. PUTNAM made in Germany; molded/painted hair, glass sleep eyes, closed mouth, flange neck, cloth body, stamped in red ink BYE-LO-BABY Pat. Appl'd For COPY BY GRACE STOREY PUTNAM; celluloid hands. 14″ long, head circumference 12½″. $475-500.

24

ALL BISQUE

Arranged alphabetically
by country of origin

AMERICAN, all painted bisque, marked STORY BOOK DOLL USA 11; mohair wig, painted features, jointed at hips and shoulders. 5″ tall, $40-50.

AMERICAN, "Nancy Ann Story Book Christening Baby," all painted bisque, marked STORY BOOK DOLL USA 2; molded/painted hair and features, jointed baby body. All original. 3½″ tall, $40-55.

AMERICAN, "Nancy Ann Story Book Doll," all painted bisque, marked STORY BOOK DOLL USA; mohair wig, molded/painted features, shoes and socks, jointed at shoulders. 5¼″ tall, $30-40.

AMERICAN(?), all stone bisque, marked L.D. Kenny Co. (ink stamp); molded/painted hair, features, and clothes; jointed at hips and shoulders. 4″ tall, $45-55.

FRENCH(?), all bisque, socket head, marked 2; mohair wig, glass sleep eyes, closed mouth, jointed at hips and shoulders, molded/painted shoes and black stockings. 8″ tall, $325-350.

FRENCH TYPE, all bisque, marked 13 on head and body; socket head, mohair wig, glass inset eyes, closed mouth; molded/painted shoes with heels and long black stockings. 5″ tall, $300-325.

FRENCH TYPE, all bisque, clothes sewed on; mohair wig, glass inset eyes, closed mouth; jointed shoulders and hips, molded/painted shoes and socks. All original. 4″ tall, $275-300.

FRENCH TYPE, all bisque, swivel head, marked 16/0; human hair wig, paperweight eyes, closed mouth, jointed shoulders and hips, molded/painted shoes and socks. 7″ tall, $300-325.

GERMAN, all bisque, swivel head, marked 4; mohair wig, glass inset eyes, closed mouth; jointed shoulders and hips, molded/painted shoes and socks. 9″ tall, $350-400.

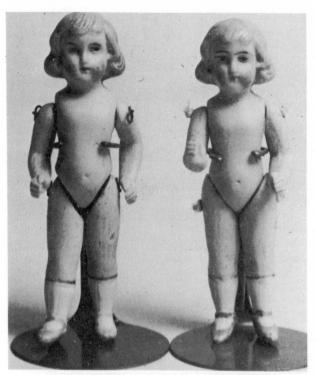

GERMAN(?), all bisque, marked 3701 1; mohair wig, glass inset eyes, open/closed mouth; jointed at shoulders and hips, molded/painted shoes and socks. 4¾″ tall, $225-250.

GERMAN, all bisque, marked 2/0; molded/painted hair and features; jointed at hips and shoulders, molded/painted shoes and socks. 3½″ tall, each $200-225.

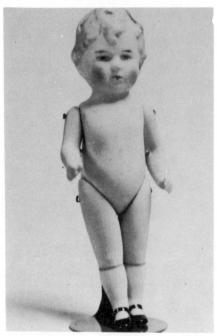

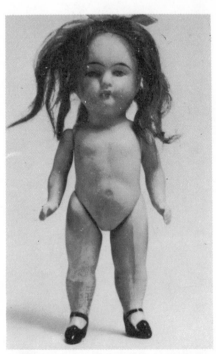

GERMAN(?), all bisque, marked "three leaf clover" P 23; molded/painted "boy style" hair and features, shoes and socks, jointed shoulders and hips. 5½″ tall, $225-250.

GERMAN, all bisque, unmarked; mohair wig, molded/painted features; jointed at shoulders with molded/painted shoes and socks. 3″ tall, $200-250.

GERMAN(?), all bisque, marked 600 over 4; mohair wig, molded/painted eyes and mouth, jointed shoulders and hips with molded/painted shoes and socks. 5½″ tall, $225-250.

GERMAN, all bisque, marked 36 5; mohair wig, inset glass eyes, (left) closed mouth, (right) open mouth, molded teeth, jointed at hips and shoulders, yellow molded/painted shoes and white socks. 5″ tall (left), $200-225. 5″ tall (right), $200-225.

GERMAN, all bisque, (left) marked 3 Germany, (right) marked 145 12; molded/painted hair and features; jointed at hips and shoulders, molded/painted shoes and socks. 5¼″ tall, each $200-225.

GERMAN, all bisque, (left) marked 5 D 3½ 10, (right) unmarked; molded/painted hair and features, jointed at hips and shoulders, molded/painted shoes and socks. 6″ and 5″ tall, each $225-250.

GERMAN, all bisque, unmarked; molded/painted hair, features, and bows, jointed at hips and shoulders. 7½″ tall, $250-275.

GERMAN, all bisque, unmarked; mohair wig, inset glass eyes, closed mouth, jointed at hips and shoulders, molded/painted shoes and socks. 4½″ tall, $200-225.

GERMAN (?), all bisque, marked 620 / 3½; sheepskin wig, molded/painted eyes and mouth; jointed shoulders and hips, molded/painted 4-button shoes and socks. 6½″ tall, $175-200.

GERMAN(?), all bisque, marked(?) (clothes sewed on); molded/painted hair and features, jointed shoulders and hips. All original. 1¾″ tall, $125-150.

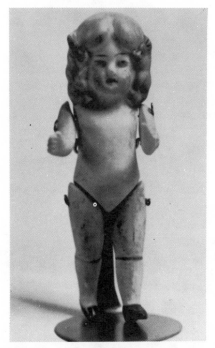

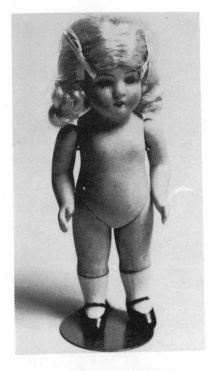

GERMAN, all bisque, marked 3 leaf clover P 14; molded/painted hair with bows, features, shoes and socks; jointed shoulders and hips. 5″ tall, $175-200.

GERMAN (?), all bisque, marked 600 over 4; mohair wig, molded/painted features, shoes and socks; jointed shoulders and hips. 6″ tall, $175-200.

GERMAN, all bisque, marked 83 over 50 Germany; mohair wig, glass sleep eyes, open mouth; jointed shoulders and hips with molded/painted shoes and socks. 5½″ tall, $250-300.

GERMAN, all bisque, marked Germany; mohair wig, glass inset eyes, closed mouth; jointed shoulders and hips, molded/painted shoes and socks. 3½" tall. $200-225.

GERMAN (?), all bisque, marked 2/0; mohair wig, molded/painted features, shoes and socks; jointed shoulders and hips. 4½" tall, $150-175.

GERMAN (?), all bisque, marked 160 over 4/0; mohair wig, glass inset eyes, closed mouth; jointed at shoulders and hips with molded/painted shoes and socks. 4¾" tall, $150-175.

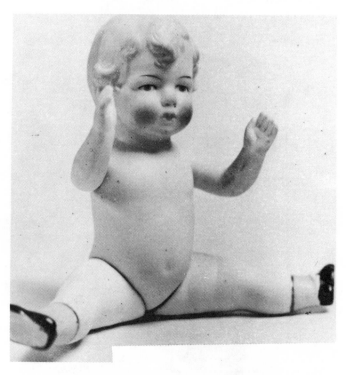

GERMAN (?), all bisque, marked 130 over 4; mohair wig, molded/painted features, shoes and socks; jointed shoulders and hips. 5¾" tall, $150-175.

GERMAN (?), all bisque, marked 653/4; molded/painted boy style hair, features, shoes and socks; jointed shoulders and hips. 7½" tall, $250-300.

30

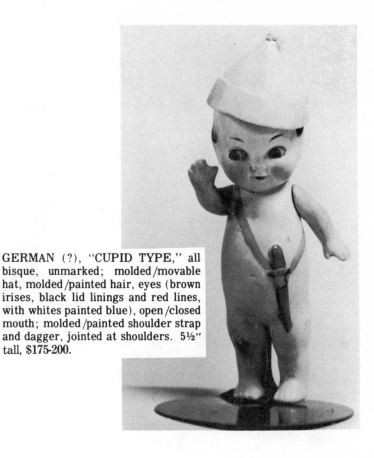

GERMAN (?), "CUPID TYPE," all bisque, unmarked; molded/movable hat, molded/painted hair, eyes (brown irises, black lid linings and red lines, with whites painted blue), open/closed mouth; molded/painted shoulder strap and dagger, jointed at shoulders. 5½" tall, $175-200.

GERMAN, all bisque, unmarked; molded/painted hair and features; jointed at hips and shoulders with molded/painted shoes and socks. 4½" tall, $125-150.

GERMAN, all bisque, marked 83 N 100; mohair wig, glass sleep eyes, open mouth; jointed at hips and shoulders with molded/painted shoes and socks. 6" tall, $275-300.

GERMAN, all brown bisque, unmarked; socket head, mohair wig, inset glass eyes, open mouth with molded teeth; jointed at hips and shoulders. 4½" tall, $350-400.

GERMAN, "CUPID'S SISTER," all bisque marked 10414 Germany; molded/painted hair (with upside down bows) and features; jointed at hips and shoulders. 5¼" tall, $175-200.

31

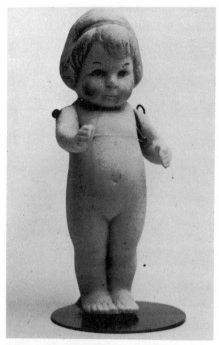  

GERMAN, all bisque, unmarked; molded/painted hair, features, and ribbon; jointed at shoulders. 4" tall, $125-150.

GERMAN, all bisque, unmarked; molded/painted hair and hat, features and shoes; jointed at shoulders. 4" tall, $125-150.

GERMAN (?), all bisque, unmarked; molded/painted hair, features, stocking cap, clothes, shoes and knee length socks; jointed at shoulders. 8" tall, $275-300.

GERMAN, "INDIAN," all bisque, mark on foot not readable; molded/painted hair, features, loin cloth and sandals. 2¼" tall, $125-150.

GERMAN, all bisque, unmarked; molded/painted hair, features, and clothes; jointed at shoulders. 5" tall, $200-225.

GERMAN, all bisque, unmarked;
molded/painted hair, features, and
clothes; jointed at hips and shoulders.
6″ tall, $150-200.

GERMAN, all bisque, marked Germany; molded/painted hair, features,
and clothes. 2¼″ tall, each $100-125.

GERMAN, all bisque, unmarked;
molded/painted hair, features, and
clothes. 2½″ tall, $125-150.

GERMAN, all bisque, (left) unmarked,
(right) marked Germany 4325; mold-
ed/painted hair, features, and clothes.
2″ and 3″ tall, each $125-150.

GERMAN, all bisque, marked Germany; molded/painted hair, features, and clothes. 2¼" tall, **each $85-100.**

GERMAN "NODDER," all bisque, marked Germany; molded/painted hair, features, bonnet, purse, clothes, and shoes. 3" tall, **$125-150.**

GERMAN "RACHEL," all bisque nodder, marked RACHEL Germany; molded/painted face, features, arms, hat and clothes; swivel/nodding head. 3½" tall, **$150-175.**

GERMAN, "ANDY GUMP," all bisque nodder, marked ANDY GUMP Germany; molded/painted features, hat and clothes; swivel/nodding head. 4" tall, **$175-200.**

GERMAN, "NODDER," all bisque, marked Germany; molded/painted hair, features, hat, clothes, shoes and socks; swivel/nodding head. 3" tall, **$125-150.**

GERMAN, "NODDERS," all bisque, unmarked; molded/painted hair, features, and clothes; jointed at neck only. 3″ tall, each $125-150.

GERMAN, "NODDER," all bisque, marked Germany; molded/painted hair, features, top hat and clothes; swivel/nodding head. 2¾″ tall, $125-150.

GERMAN, "NODDERS," all bisque, (left) marked 11016, (right) marked "Chubby Chaney" Germany; molded/painted hair, features, and clothes; jointed at neck only. 3½″ tall, (left), $150-175. 3½″ tall (right), $225-250.

GERMAN, "NODDERS," all bisque, (left) unmarked, (right) marked Germany; molded/painted hair, features, and clothes; jointed at neck only. 3¼″ tall, each $125-150.

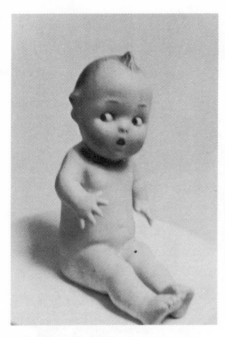

GERMAN, all bisque, marked HEU-BACH (in a square) 9748 4; molded/painted hair and features. 5″ tall, $350-400.

GERMAN (?), all bisque, marked A. R. 808; molded/painted hair and features, open/closed mouth with two teeth. 3″ tall, $125-150.

GERMAN, all bisque, marked 874; molded/painted hair, features and clothes. 3″ tall, $175-200.

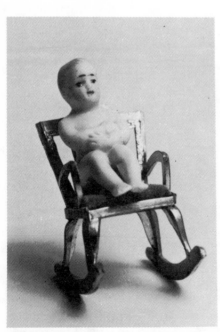

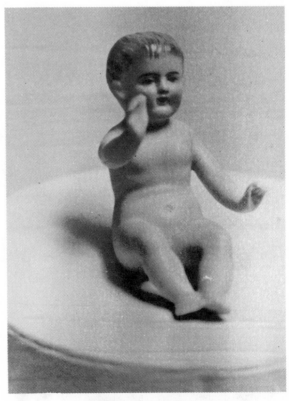

GERMAN, all bisque, unmarked; molded/painted hair and features. 2¼″ tall, $100-125.

GERMAN (?), all bisque, marked 3/0; molded/painted hair and features. 2¾″ tall, $125-150.

GERMAN, "SNOW BABIES," all bisque, (left) unmarked, (right) marked Germany (ink stamp); molded/painted features with molded snowsuit. 2½" tall, $175-200. 1¼" tall, $125-150.

GERMAN, all pink bisque, marked Germany; molded/painted hair and features; jointed at hips and shoulders with molded/painted shoes and socks. Left (top and bottom) original costumes. 2" tall, each $85-100.

GERMAN, all pink bisque, marked Germany; molded/painted hair (with hole to insert ribbon) and features; jointed at shoulders. 2½" tall, $125-150.

GERMAN, "SNOW BABIES," all bisque (left and middle) marked Germany (ink stamp), (right) unmarked; molded/painted features with molded snowsuit. 1" and 1½" tall, each $125-150. 2" tall, $150-175.

GERMAN, all pink bisque, marked
Germany; molded/painted hair and
features; (left and right) jointed at
shoulders, (middle) unjointed with
molded clothes. 2¼″ tall, each $100-125.
1½″ tall, $85-100.

GERMAN, all pink bisque, marked 943
Germany 7½; molded/painted hair and
features; jointed at hips and shoulders.
3¼″ tall, $100-125.

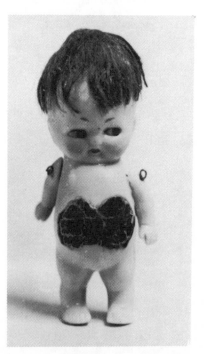

GERMAN, all pink bisque, unmarked;
molded/painted hair and features;
jointed at hips and shoulders with
molded/painted shoes and socks. 4½″
tall, each $125-150.

GERMAN, all bisque, marked Germany; molded/painted hair and features, jointed at shoulders. 4½″ tall,
$125-150.

GERMAN, all bisque, marked Germany; mohair wig, molded/painted
features, jointed at shoulders. 3¼″
tall, $100-125.

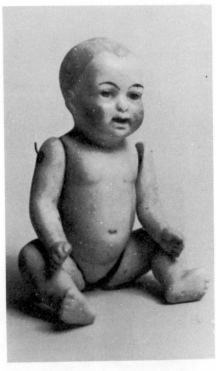

GERMAN, all bisque, marked R A; molded/painted hair and features, jointed at shoulders. 3″ tall, $100-125.

GERMAN, all bisque, unmarked; molded/painted hair and features; jointed at hips and shoulders. 4½″ long, $125-150.

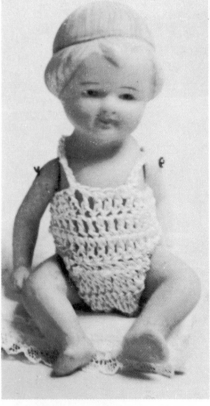

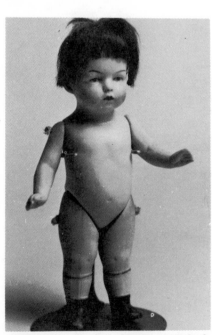

GERMAN, all bisque, unmarked; molded/painted hair with blue ribbon and features; jointed baby body. 5″ tall, $100-125.

GERMAN, all pink bisque, marked 620/3½; mohair wig, molded/painted features; jointed at hips and shoulders with molded/painted shoes and socks. 6¼″ tall, $150-175.

GERMAN, all pink bisque, unmarked; molded/painted hair and features, jointed at shoulders. 5″ tall, $175-200.

GERMAN, all painted bisque, marked
Germany 5575; molded/painted hair
and features; jointed at hips and shoulders with molded/painted shoes and
socks. All original. 7″ tall, $125-150.

GERMAN, all bisque, marked Germany; molded/painted hair and features; jointed at hips and shoulders.
3″ long, $85-100.

GERMAN, all painted bisque, marked
Germany; molded/painted hair and
features; jointed at hips and shoulders
with painted shoes. All original "Shak-
er" costumes. 6″ tall, pair $175-200.

GERMAN, all painted bisque, marked
Germany (ink stamp on foot); molded/
painted hair and features; jointed at
hips and shoulders. All original. 3¼″
tall, each $85-100.

40

GERMAN, all painted bisque, marked
Germany 5575; molded/painted hair
and features; jointed at hips and shoulders with molded/painted shoes and
socks. 7″ tall, **each $100-125.**

JAPANESE bride and groom, all stone
bisque, marked JAPAN; molded/
painted hair and features; jointed at
shoulders. 3″ tall, **pair $50-60.**

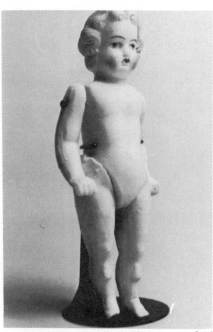

GERMAN, all stone bisque, marked
250 0 Germany; mohair wig, molded/
painted features, shoes and socks with
tassels; jointed at shoulders. 3½″ tall,
$150-175.

GERMAN, all stone bisque, marked
280 4; molded/painted hair and features; jointed at hips and shoulders.
5″ tall, **$100-125.**

JAPANESE, all bisque, marked
JAPAN; molded/painted hair, features
clothes, shoes, socks. 3½″ tall, **$40-50.**

JAPANESE all stone bisque, marked JAPAN; molded/painted hair, features, hat, clothes and shoes. 3½″ tall, $40-50.

JAPANESE, all bisque, marked NIPPON; molded/painted hair, features and clothes. 3¾″ tall, $85-100.

JAPANESE all bisque, marked JOLLIKID NIPPON (on sticker); molded/painted hair, features, and clothes; jointed at shoulders. 3½″ tall, $50-75.

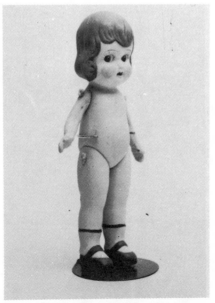

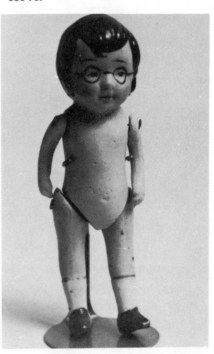

JAPANESE, all stone bisque, marked MADE IN JAPAN; molded/painted hair and features; jointed at shoulders. 7″ tall, $50-60.

JAPANESE, all stone bisque, marked MADE IN JAPAN; molded/painted hair and features; jointed at hips and shoulders with molded/painted shoes and socks. 8½″ tall, $60-70.

JAPANESE, all bisque, marked MADE IN JAPAN; molded/painted hair, features and glasses; jointed at hips and shoulders with molded/painted shoes and socks. 5″ tall, $60-70.

JAPANESE (?), "KEWPIE," all bisque, marked RW384; molded/painted hair, features, shoes and socks. 5″ tall, $40-50.

JAPANESE, all bisque, marked NIPPON; molded/painted hair and features with open/closed mouth; jointed at hips and shoulders. 5″ long, $60-70.

JAPANESE (?), all bisque, unmarked; mohair wisps of hair, glass sleep eyes, closed mouth; jointed at shoulders, paper squeaker on stomach; molded/painted shoes and socks. 6¼″ tall, $40-50.

JAPANESE (?), all fine quality stone bisque, marked SHINOOA (indistinguishable symbol); painted hair, molded/painted features; jointed at hips and shoulders, painted shoes. Original costumes. 4″ tall, **pair $60-70**.

JAPANESE, all brown stone bisque, marked MADE IN JAPAN; wisps of hair inserted in three holes in head, molded/painted features; brown jointed baby body. 4″ long, $40-50.

JAPANESE, all brown painted bisque, marked MADE IN JAPAN; mohair pigtails, molded/painted features; jointed at hips and shoulders. 4¼″ tall, $50-60.

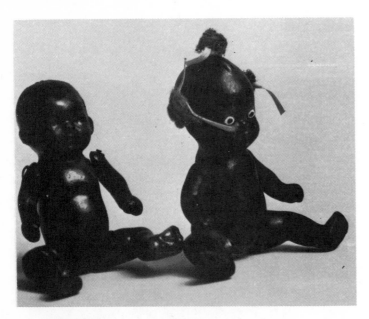

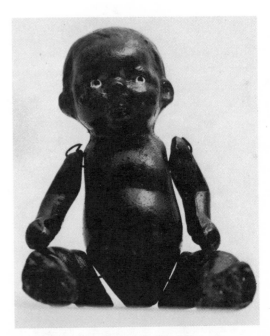

JAPANESE, all brown painted bisque, (left) marked # MADE IN JAPAN; molded/painted hair and features; (right) marked MADE IN JAPAN, mohair pigtails, painted features; both jointed at hips and shoulders, 3½″ and 4″ tall, **each $40-50.**

JAPANESE, all brown painted bisque, marked JAPAN; molded/painted hair and features; jointed at hips and shoulders. 4½″ tall, $40-50.

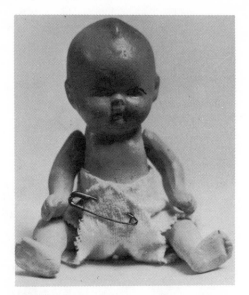

JAPANESE, all stone bisque, marked MADE IN JAPAN; molded/painted hair and features; jointed baby body. 3½″ long, $30-40.

KESTNER, all bisque; marked 150 over 2, (paper label) Crown w/KEST-NER Germany; mohair wig, glass sleep eyes, open mouth with four teeth, jointed shoulders and hips with molded/painted shoes and socks. 8″ tall, $375-400.

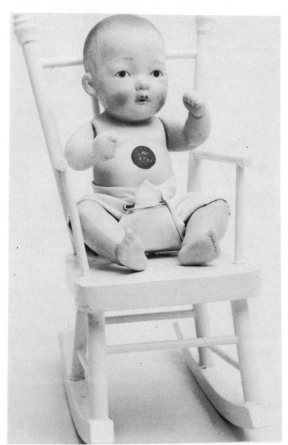

JAPANESE, all bisque, body incised and sticker reads Made in Japan; jointed at hips and shoulders, painted hair, painted eyes, closed mouth. 7″ head circumference, 8″ long, $70-80.

KESTNER, all bisque, unmarked except KESTNER crown sticker; mohair wig, glass sleep eyes, open mouth with molded teeth; jointed at hips and shoulders with molded/painted shoes and socks. 7″ tall, $375-400.

KEWPIE BISQUES

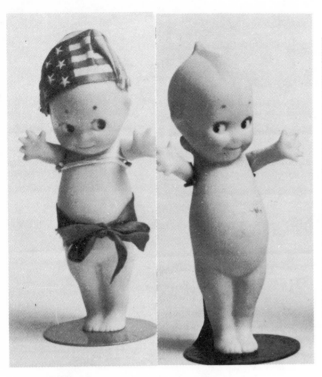

KEWPIE, all bisque, unmarked; molded/painted hair and features; jointed at shoulders. 4¼" tall, **each $175-200.**

KEWPIE, "HUGGERS" and "SCHOLAR," all bisque, unmarked; molded/painted hair and features. 2¼" tall (left), $275-300. 2" tall (right), $250-300.

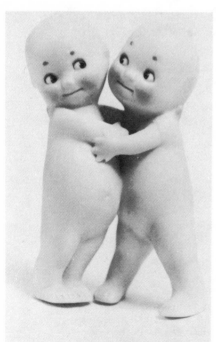

KEWPIE, "BUTTONHOLE," all bisque, unmarked; molded/painted features. 2" tall, $200-225.

KEWPIE, "HUGGERS," all bisque, unmarked; molded/painted hair and features. 3½" tall, $300-325.

KEWPIE, "ROSE O'NEILL," all bisque; marked O'NEILL (on feet), KEWPIE Germany (on sticker), ROSE O'NEILL Copyright (sticker on back); molded/painted hair and features, jointed at shoulders. 4" tall, $200-250.

KEWPIE, "ROSE O'NEILL," all bisque; marked O'NEILL (on feet), KEWPIE Germany (on sticker); molded/painted hair and features, jointed at shoulders. 6½" tall, $200-225. 5¼" tall, $225-250.

WOLF, LOUIS & CO., "CHUBBY," all bisque, marked (left) CHUBBY L. W. & Co. Germany, (right) CHUBBY L. W. & CO. Nippon; molded/painted hair, features, and clothes. 6½" tall, $300-350. 4½" tall, $180-230.

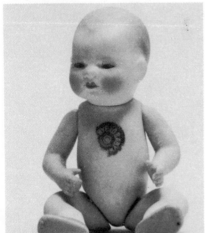

PUTNAM, GRACE STOREY, "BYE-LO," all bisque; swivel head with 13 incised on neck flange, molded/painted hair, glass sleep brown eyes, closed mouth; jointed baby body marked BYE-LO BABY c (in a circle) Germany (GRACE S. PUTNAM part missing) (on dark green sticker); 6—13 Copr. by Grace S. Putnam incised on back, 6 over 13 incised on arms, 894/13 incised on leg flanges; molded/painted blue shoes and white socks. 5" long, 4¾" head circumference, $450-500.

NIPPON, "WIDE-AWAKE," all bisque; marked NIPPON; molded/painted hair and features, open/closed mouth; jointed at shoulders with molded/painted shoes and socks. 6" tall, $80-100. 5" tall, $70-95.

47

AMERICAN BISQUE

FULPER POTTERY COMPANY, bisque, socket head; marked FULPER (incised vertically) MADE IN U S A, HORSMAN DOLL 19c10; mohair wig, glass sleep eyes, open mouth with oscillating tongue; mache jointed baby body. 20″ long, 15″ head circumference, $500-550.

FULPER POTTERY COMPANY, bisque, socket head; marked FULPER (in vertical oval) made in U.S.A. 20; mohair wig, glass sleep eyes, open mouth; mache/wood jointed body. 20″ tall, $375-400.

CELLULOID DOLLS

Arranged
by manufacturer

BUSCHOW & BECK (?), celluloid, swivel head, molded/painted hair, inset glass eyes, closed mouth; celluloid jointed body marked (a helmet) Minerva. 12½" tall, $125-150; 18½" tall, $150-175.

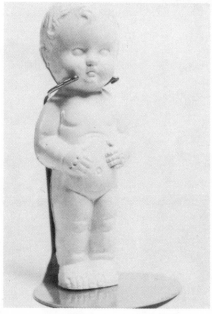

COMPANY UNIDENTIFIED, all celluloid, marked patent NO.12574 No. 12575; molded/painted features, legs push into body, squeaker. 5" tall, $35-45.

BEST & COMPANY, all celluloid, marked BEST U.S.A.; molded hair, features and body. 3" tall, $25-35.

BUSCHOW & BECK (?), celluloid shoulder-head, marked (a helmet) Germany To2 8ct; molded/painted hair, inset glass eyes, closed mouth; cloth body with celluloid hands. 10½" tall, $65-75.

COMPANY UNIDENTIFIED, celluloid shoulder-head, marked Made in France; molded/painted hair, inset celluloid eyes, open/closed mouth; all cloth body. 15½" tall, $125-150.

COMPANY UNIDENTIFIED, all celluloid baby; jointed at hips and shoulders, molded/painted hair, painted eyes, closed mouth. Body marked CVO (superimposed in a circle) U.S.A. 7" long, $35-45.

COMPANY UNIDENTIFIED, all celluloid, jointed at hips and shoulders, molded/painted features and clothes. Marked JAPAN. 3" tall, each $20-30.

COMPANY UNIDENTIFIED, celluloid head, hands, and feet, molded/painted features; cloth body stuffed with excelsior. Marked JAPAN. 8" tall, each $35-45.

COMPANY UNIDENTIFIED, all celluloid, jointed at shoulders, molded/painted features. Marked (a butterfly) Made in Japan. 6″ tall, **each $25-35.**

FRENCH "PROVENCAL DOLLS," all celluloid, jointed at hips and shoulders, mohair wig, painted eyes, closed mouth. 4″ and 6″ tall, **each $50-60.**

IRWIN PLASTICS, all celluloid boy, marked IRWIN Made in U.S.A. 4½; molded/painted hair and features. 4¼" tall, $20-30.

PARSONS-JACKSON COMPANY, all Biskoline (resembles celluloid), socket head marked "raised stork"; bald head, molded/painted features; jointed baby body marked "raised stork" PARSONS-JACKSON CO. Cleveland, Ohio U.S.A.; body held together with oil tempered steel springs. 10" long, 7½" head circumference, $250-275.

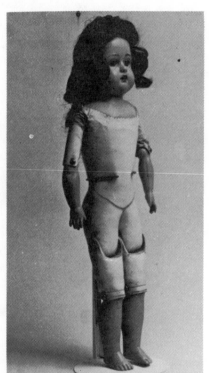

RHEINISCHE GUMMI, for KAMMER & RHEINHART, celluloid shoulder head marked K (star) R 255 (turtle in a diamond); human wig, glass sleep eyes, open mouth; oilcloth jointed body with celluloid arms and legs. 20½" tall, $225-250.

RHEINISCHE GUMMI, for KATHE KRUSE, celluloid socket head marked turtle in a diamond; human hair wig, inset celluloid eyes (lids sleep over eyes), closed mouth, celluloid jointed body. All original including tag. 16" tall, $175-200.

UNMARKED, celluloid head, molded/painted hair, painted eyes, closed mouth, all velveteen stuffed body. 13" tall, $40-50.

RHEINISCHE GUMMI, celluloid shoulder head marked turtle in a diamond; human hair wig, inset glass eyes, open mouth, cloth body with celluloid arms. All original Swedish costume. 11″ tall, **pair $250-275.**

UNMARKED, all celluloid, molded/painted features and clothes, jointed at shoulders. 6″ tall, $30-40.

UNMARKED, "CARNIVAL DOLL," all celluloid; molded/painted hair, features, shoes and socks; jointed at shoulders. 12″ tall, $30-40.

CHINA HEAD DOLLS

*Arranged according
to date*

1830s BIEDERMEIER TYPE, china-shoulder-head; human hair wig, blue painted eyes; cloth body with china arms and legs. 19″ tall, $1,700-1,900.

1830s BIEDERMEIER TYPE, china-shoulder-head; human hair wig, blue painted eyes, cloth body with china arms. 24″ tall, $1,900-2,200.

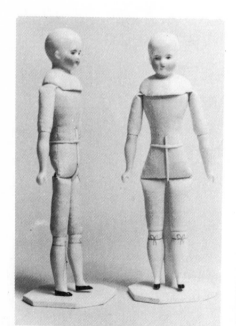

1830s BIEDERMEIER TYPE, china-shoulder-head; wig missing, blue painted eyes, cloth body with china arms and legs. 9″ tall, each $900-1,000.

1830s BIEDERMEIER TYPE, china-shoulder-head; light creamy tint; mohair wig, blue painted eyes, cloth body with china arms and legs. 18″ tall, $1,700-1,900.

1830s BIEDERMEIER TYPE, china-shoulder-head, light flesh tint; human hair wig, blue painted eyes, cloth body with china arms and legs. 15½″ tall, $1,900-2,200.

1840s TYPE, china-shoulder-head, pink tint; brown painted eyes, cloth body with kid arms. 27″ tall, $1,600-1,800.

1840s TYPE, china-shoulder-head, slight pink tint; blue painted eyes, cloth body with kid arms. 23½″ tall, $1,200-1,400.

1840s TYPE, china-shoulder-head, pink tint; blue painted eyes, cloth body with china arms and legs. 17½″ tall, $1,100-1,300.

1840s TYPE, china-shoulder-head; brown painted eyes, cloth body with kid arms, individually stitched/wired fingers. 14″ tall, $1,600-1,800.

1850s TYPE, JENNY LIND, china-shoulder-head, creamy tint; brown painted eyes, cloth body with kid hands and feet. 16″ tall, $1,800-2,000.

1840s TYPE, china-shoulder-head, pink tint; blue painted eyes, cloth body with china arms and legs. 14″ tall, $1,200-1,400.

1850-60s TYPE, china-shoulder-head; blue painted eyes, cloth body with china arms and legs. 4¼" tall, $150-175.

1850-60s TYPE, china-shoulder-head, flesh tint; brown painted eyes, molded lids, lower lashes, exposed ears, cloth body with china hands on kid arms. 20" tall, $2,500-3,000.

1850-60s TYPE, china-shoulder-head, creamy tint; brown painted eyes, molded lids, lower lashes, smiling mouth, cloth body with kid arms. 27½" tall, $3,500-4,000.

1850 to 60s TYPE, china-shoulder-head, marked 1845 (in black under glaze) on lower part of back left shoulder; light flesh tint, blue painted eyes, cloth body with kid arms and feet. 25½" tall, $2,500-3,000.

1850-60s TYPE, JENNY LIND, china-shoulder-head; blue painted eyes, molded lids; cloth body marked Patd. Dec. 15, 1885; china arms, Philip Goldsmith body. 22" tall, $2,500-3,000.

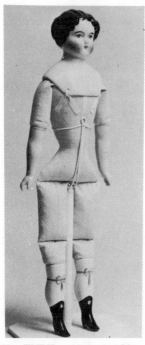

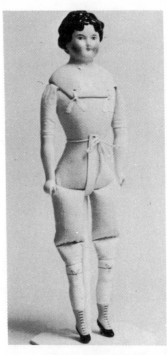

1850-60s TYPE, china-shoulder-head; blue painted eyes, cloth body with china arms and legs. 16½" tall, $600-650.

1850-60s TYPE, china-shoulder-head; blue painted eyes, molded lids, cloth body with china arms and legs. 11½" tall, $600-650.

1870s TYPE, "DOLLY MADISON," china-shoulder-head, black molded bow, gray-white china; blue painted eyes, cloth body with china arms and legs. 17" tall, $750-850.

1870s TYPE, "DOLLY MADISON," china-turned-shoulder-head, molded/painted blue ribbon with bow in hair, flesh tint; blue painted eyes, cloth body with kid hands. 23" tall, $1,000-1,300.

1870s TYPE, SPILL CURL, china-shoulder-head; blue painted eyes, molded lids, exposed ears, cloth body with kid arms. 21" tall, $1,500-1,800.

1870s TYPE, CURLY TOP, china-shoulder-head; blue painted eyes, kid body with wax over mache arms. 18" tall, $800-900.

1870s TYPE, "MRS. BUMBLEBOT-TOM," china-shoulder-head; blue painted eyes, exposed ears, cloth body with china arms and legs. 16½" tall, $600-650.

1880s TYPE, china-shoulder-head, white china; blue painted eyes, cloth body with china hands and feet. 13½" tall, $275-300.

1880s TYPE, china-shoulder-head; blue painted eyes, exposed ears, cloth body with china arms and legs. 19" tall, $600-650.

1880s TYPE, china-shoulder-head, white china; blue painted eyes, cloth body with china arms and legs. 5" tall, $100-125.

1880s TYPE, china-shoulder-head; blue painted eyes, cloth body with china arms and legs. 16½" tall, $400-450.

1880s TYPE, china-shoulder-head; blue painted eyes, cloth body with china arms and legs. 18" tall, $375-400.

1880s TYPE, china-shoulder-head, white china; blue painted eyes, cloth body with china hands and feet. 10" tall, $225-250.

1880s TYPE, china-shoulder-head, white china; blue painted eyes, cloth body with china arms and legs. 16½" tall, $375-400.

1880-90s TYPE, "HIGHLAND MARY," china-shoulder-head; blue painted eyes, cloth body with china arms and legs. 12½" tall, $450-500.

1890s TYPE, C. F. KLING & COMPANY, china-shoulder-head, marked Germany 189 K (in a bell) 7, pink tint; blue painted eyes, cloth body with china arms and legs. 19" tall, $525-550.

1920s TYPE, JAPANESE, china-shoulder-head, white china; blue painted eyes, cloth body with china arms and legs. 12″ tall, $200-225.

1890s TYPE, C. F. KLING & COMPANY, china-shoulder-head, marked Germany 189 K (in a bell) 7, pink tint; blue painted eyes, cloth body with china arms and legs. 20½″ tall, $425-450.

1920s TYPE, JAPANESE, china-shoulder-head, white china; blue painted eyes, cloth body with china arms and legs. 12″ tall, $200-225.

CHINA Frozen Charlottes, Frozen Charlies

CHARLOTTE IN A TUB, pink china with molded/painted features in white china tub. 1¼″ and 2″, each $150-200.

FROZEN CHARLOTTES; three black Charlottes are unglazed with molded hair and features; white Charlotte is white china with painted hair and features. 1″ down to ½″ tall, each $20-30.

FROZEN CHARLOTTES, white china (left), molded/painted hair (1850s type) and features, gold lustre shoes; pink tint china (right), molded/painted hair (1840s type) and features. 2″ and 1½″ tall, each $125-150.

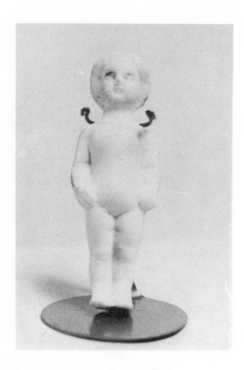

FROZEN CHARLOTTE, unglazed, molded hair and features with painted eyebrows. 3″ tall, $30-35.

FINE QUALITY CHARLOTTES; pink tint china couple (upper left), boy has painted hair with brush marks, girl has molded white china bonnet with blue bow under chin; bisque girl (top), glazed blond hair, molded robe; pink tint china (far upper right) has blue trim molded tunic; others, white china with molded/painted features and/or clothes. 2-4½″ tall, **each $150-175.**

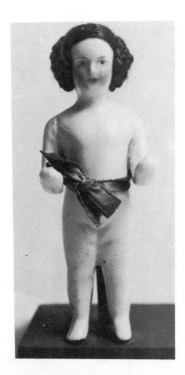

FROZEN CHARLOTTE, unglazed, mohair wig, painted features. 3¼″ tall, $85-100.

CHARLOTTE, white china, mohair wig, painted features. 4″ tall, $150-175.

CHARLOTTE, white china, molded/painted hair (1850s type) and features. 4¼″ tall, $125-150.

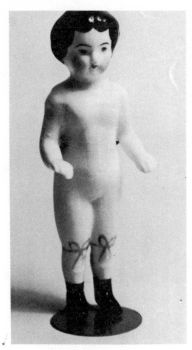

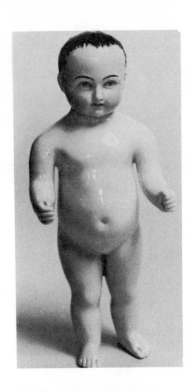

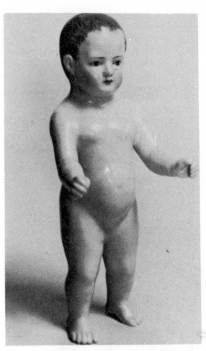

CHARLOTTE, white china, molded/painted hair (1850s type) and features. 5½″ tall, $125-150.

FROZEN CHARLIE, flesh tint face; molded/painted boy style hair, molded eyelids, painted features, white china body. 11½″ tall, $525-575.

FROZEN CHARLIE, all over flesh tint; molded/painted boy style hair, painted features. 14″ tall, $550-600.

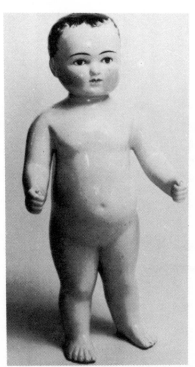

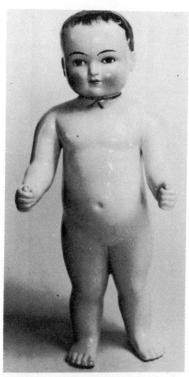

FROZEN CHARLIE, flesh tint face; molded/painted boy style hair, painted features, white china body. 15½″ tall, $700-800.

FROZEN CHARLIE, flesh tint face; molded/painted boy style hair, painted features, blue tie, white china body. 16½″ tall, $850-900.

FROZEN CHARLIE, flesh tint face; molded/painted boy style hair, painted features, white china body. 16½″ tall, $850-900.

CHINA, heads only

Arranged according to date

1850-60s TYPE, (right) creamy china.
3″ tall (left), $125-150; 2½″ tall (right),
$100-125.

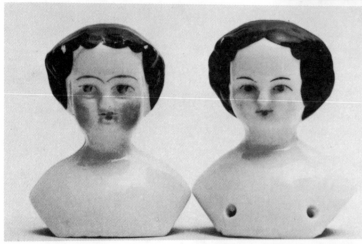

1850-60s TYPE. 2½″ tall, **each $85-
100.**

1850-60s TYPE, (right) turned head.
6″ tall, **each $225-250.**

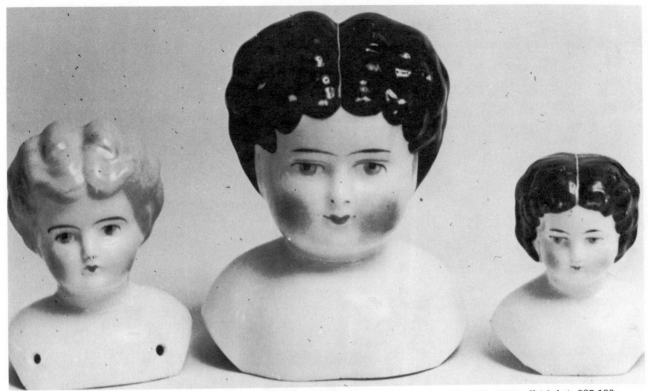

1880s TYPE, 1860s TYPE (right). 3″ tall (left), $100-125; 4″ tall (middle), $125-150; 2½″ tall (right), $85-100.

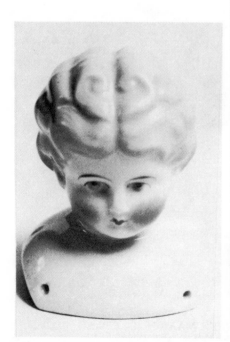  

1880s TYPE, china-shoulder-head, white china, blue painted eyes. 4½″ tall, $125-150.

1880s TYPE, china-shoulder-head, white china, blue painted eyes. 3½″ tall, $125-150.

1880s TYPE, china-shoulder-head, white china, blue painted eyes. 2″ tall, $100-125.

1880s TYPE. 5″ tall (left), $200-225. 5″ tall (right), $200-225.

1880s TYPE (left), turned head; 1850-60s TYPE (right), slight pink tint. 5″ tall (left), $225-250. 6¼″ tall (right), $250-275.

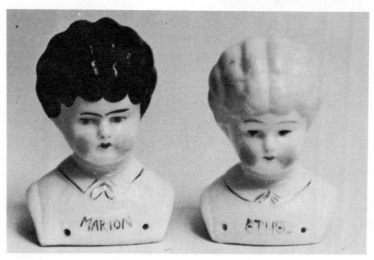

1880s TYPE, MARION & ETHEL, marked PATENT APP'D FOR Germany. 3″ tall, each $150-175.

CLOTH DOLLS

UNMARKED, molded cloth head covered with silk stockinet, mohair wig, painted eyes, cloth body with mache hands. 26″ tall, **pair $350-400.**

KAMKINS, molded cloth head; mohair wig, oil painted features, all cloth body, jointed at hips and shoulders. 21″ tall, $200-225.

CHASE, MARTHA J., BOY, cloth stockinet head; molded/oil painted hair and features, molded ears, early pink sateen covered cloth body with oil painted stockinet arms and legs. 18½″ tall, $200-225.

CHASE, MARTHA J., BABY, cloth stockinet head; molded/oil painted hair and features, molded ears, sateen covered cloth body with oil painted stockinet arms and legs. 26″ tall, $250-275.

CHASE (?) (similar to Martha Chase except a finer finish), cloth stockinet head; mohair wig, molded/oil painted features, molded ears, sateen body with oil painted stockinet arms and legs. 20½″ tall, $200-225.

CHASE, MARTHA J., TODDLER, cloth stockinet head; molded/oil painted hair and features, molded ears, sateen covered cloth body with oil painted stockinet arms and legs. 16½″ tall, $225-250.

KRUGER, R. G., DWARFS, molded mask face with painted features, velveteen body; tag reads AUTHENTIC WALT DISNEY CHARACTER, exclusive with R.G. KRUGER New York. 12″ tall, each $75-100.

LENCI, all felt, swivel head; yarn-like hair sewed into felt in rows, molded/painted features with side glancing eyes; body jointed shoulders and hips. Paper tag on dress, MODELLO DEPOSITATO LENCI TORINO made in Italy. All original. 19″ tall, $225-250.

LENCI, molded felt head, mohair wig, painted eyes; felt straw stuffed body, jointed at hips and shoulders. All original. Boy marked #300J, girl's tag missing. 18″ tall, each $225-250.

LENCI, molded felt head, mohair wig, painted eyes; felt straw stuffed body, jointed at hips and shoulders. All original including tags. Marked boy #300/10, girl #300/34. 18″ tall, each $225-250.

LENCI, TROUBADOUR & DANCER, all felt, swivel head; molded/painted hair and features, body jointed shoulders and hips, stitched knee. Paper tag says LENCI di E. SCAVINI Made in Italy N 161. All original. 25″ tall, **each $250-275.**

LENCI, FLAPPER, molded felt head, painted eyes; felt straw stuffed body, jointed at hips and shoulders. Original costume. 25″ tall, $250-275.

UNMARKED, early molded cloth head, molded/painted hair (1840s type), painted eyes, all cloth body. 21″ tall, $325-350.

UNMARKED, GERMAN PEASANT GIRL, cloth head; molded/oil painted features, cloth body. All original. 12″ tall, $150-175.

UNMARKED, all printed cloth boy with printed clothes. Box in hip pocket marked QUAKER CRACKELS. 15″ tall, $100-125.

UNMARKED, ORPHAN ANNIE, all cloth doll with painted features, mohair wig. All original. 16½″ tall, $100-125.

UNMARKED, all printed cloth doll with printed clothes. Marked on body, My Name is Miss Flaked Rice. 25½″ tall, $100-125.

WALKER, IZANNAH, molded cloth shoulder-head, oil painted hair and features, all cloth body with oil painted hands. 16½″ tall, $1,500-1,800.

UNMARKED, all printed cloth doll. 11″ tall, $60-70.

WELLINGS, NORAH, JACK TAR, felt head, molded/painted features, all cloth body; marked on foot, Made in England by Norah Wellings. 10½″ tall, $60-70.

70

COMPOSITION DOLLS

Arranged
by manufacturer

ALEXANDER DOLL COMPANY, compo swivel head, marked MADAME ALEXANDER SONJA HENIE; mohair wig, glass-like eyes, open mouth; compo jointed body. 17½" tall, $125-150.

ALEXANDER DOLL COMPANY, compo swivel head, marked PRINCESS ELIZABETH ALEXANDER DOLL CO.; mohair wig, glass-like sleep eyes, open mouth, compo jointed body. 17" tall, $125-150.

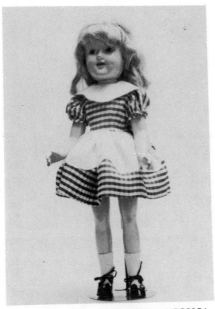

ALEXANDER, MADAME, "SONJA HENIE," all compo, swivel head, marked MADAME ALEXANDER SONJA HENIE; mohair wig, plastic sleep eyes, open mouth, body jointed shoulders and hips. 18" tall, $125-150.

ALEXANDER DOLL COMPANY, compo swivel head, marked MADAME ALEXANDER SONJA HENIE; mohair wig, glass-like sleep eyes, open mouth, compo jointed body. 21" tall, $125-150.

ALEXANDER, MADAME, all compo, swivel head, marked X (in a circle); human hair wig, plastic sleep eyes, open mouth; body marked 13, jointed shoulders and hips. 13" tall, 100-125.

ALEXANDER, MADAME, "DIONNE QUINTS," all compo, swivel head, marked "DIONNE" ALEXANDER; molded/painted hair, plastic sleep eyes, open/closed mouth; jointed baby body marked MADAME ALEXANDER. All original, mint condition. 10″ long, 9½″ head circumference, set $550-600.

ALEXANDER DOLL COMPANY, compo flange head, marked MADAME ALEXANDER; molded/painted hair, glass-like sleep eyes, open mouth; cloth body with compo arms and legs. All original. 24″ tall, $125-150.

AMBERG, LOUIS, & SON, VANTA
BABY, compo shoulder-head, marked
VANTA BABY AMBERG; molded/
painted hair, metal sleep eyes, open/
closed mouth; cloth body/compo arms
and legs. 14″ long, 10″ head circumference, $125-150.

CAMEO DOLL PROD. COMPANY,
KEWPIES, all compo; molded/paint-
ed hair and features; paper label
KEWPIE Reg. U.S. Pat. Off., on body;
sticker on bottom of feet, ROSE
O'NEILL 1913 KEWPIES—REG-U S-
PAT.-OFF-DES-PAT-III-4-1913; joint-
ed at shoulders. 9″ tall, $150-200.

ARRANBEE DOLL COMPANY, all
compo, swivel head, marked R & B;
mohair wig, plastic sleep eyes, closed
mouth; body jointed shoulder and
hips. 18″ tall, $100-125.

CAMEO DOLL PROD. COMPANY,
KEWPIES, all compo; jointed at shoulders, molded/painted hair, painted
eyes, closed mouth, legs together on
pedestal. Label on pedestal reads CO.
ROSE O'NEILL. 1913. 12½″ tall, **each**
$200-225.

CAMEO DOLL PROD. COMPANY,
KEWPIES, all compo; jointed at shoulders, molded/painted hair, painted
eyes, closed mouth, Kewpie label on
body. 11″ tall (left), $200-225. 11″ tall
(right, $225-250.

CAMEO DOLL PROD. COMPANY, "SCOOTLES," compo swivel head; molded/painted hair, painted eyes, closed mouth; compo jointed baby body. 14½" tall, $150-175.

CAMEO DOLL PROD. COMPANY, compo swivel head, painted hair, painted eyes, closed mouth; compo body with wood jointed arms and legs. Label on body reads BETTY BOOP. 12½" tall, $150-175.

CHANGE-O-DOLL COMPANY, FAM-LEE DOLL, interchangeable compo heads, unmarked; one with mohair wig and molded/painted features (smiling face); one with molded/painted hair and features (crying face); brass screw coupling inside neck; cloth body/threaded neck plug (for interchanging heads); compo arms and legs. 16" tall, $175-200.

COMPANY UNIDENTIFIED, MAE STARR, RECORD DOLL, compo shoulder-head marked MAE STARR DOLL; human hair wig, metal sleep eyes, open mouth; cloth body with phonograph mechanism, compo arms and legs. All original. 28" tall, $300-325.

COMPANY UNIDENTIFIED, NAN-CY, all compo, swivel head, marked NANCY; human hair wig, plastic sleep eyes, open mouth; body jointed shoulders and hips. 16½" tall, $70-80.

DOLL CRAFT NOVELTY CORPORA-TION, "LONE RANGER," compo flange head; molded/painted hair, painted eyes, closed mouth; cloth body with compo hands and feet. All original with tag. 16½" tall, $125-150.

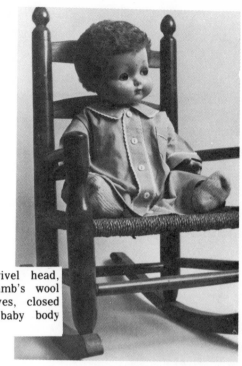

EFFANBEE, compo swivel head, marked EFFANBEE; lamb's wool wig, glass-like flirty eyes, closed mouth; compo jointed baby body 20" long, $100-125.

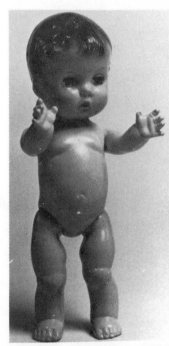

EFFANBEE, compo swivel head; molded/painted hair, painted eyes, closed mouth; compo jointed body marked PATSY JR. EFFANBEE DOLL. 11½" tall, $50-75.

EFFANBEE, compo swivel head; molded/painted hair, painted eyes, closed mouth; compo jointed body marked EFF AND BEE. All original with tag. 17" tall, $75-100.

EFFANBEE DOLL COMPANY, "CANDY KID," all compo, swivel head marked EFFANBEE, molded/painted hair, plastic sleep eyes, closed mouth; toddler body marked EFFAN-BEE; jointed shoulders and hips. 12½" tall, $50-75.

EFFANBEE, "SKIPPY," compo swivel head marked EFFANBEE SKIPPY c (in circle) P. L. CROSBY; molded/painted hair and features, cloth body/compo arms and legs, molded/painted shoes and stockings. 14" tall, $125-150.

FREUNDLICH NOVELTY CORPORTION, all compo, jointed at hips and shoulders; molded/painted hat, painted eyes, closed mouth. Tag reads "Gen. MacArthur, The Man of the Hour." All original. 18½" tall, $150-175.

HEIRLOOM NEEDLEWORK GUILD, INC., McCALL-PEGGY, all compo; jointed at shoulders, molded/painted hair, painted eyes, closed mouth. 12" tall, $65-80.

HORSMAN DOLLS, INC., "BABY BUMPS," brown compo head marked E. I. H. c (in a circle); brown bald head, molded/painted features, flange neck; cloth body/compo hands, brown sateen legs, cloth label on body, Copyright 1910 by E. I. HORSMAN. 12" long, 9" head circumference, $125-150.

HORSMAN DOLLS, INC., compo flange head; painted hair, metal sleep eyes, closed mouth; cloth body with compo arms and legs. All original. 12" long, 9" head circumference, $75-100.

HORSMAN DOLLS, INC., compo shoulder-head marked E. I. H. Co., INC.; molded/painted hair, metal sleep eyes, closed mouth; cloth body/ compo arms and legs. All original. 13″ tall, $65-85.

IDEAL TOY CORPORATION, "SHIRLEY TEMPLE," all compo, swivel head marked SHIRLEY TEMPLE large "C"/OP inside IDEAL N & T CO.; mohair wig, plastic sleep eyes, open mouth; body marked SHIRLEY TEMPLE; jointed shoulders and hips. All original. 19½″ tall, $150-175.

IDEAL TOY COMPANY, compo swivel head; mohair wig, glass-like flirty eyes, open mouth; compo jointed body marked SHIRLEY TEMPLE IDEAL DOLL CO. All original. 27½″ tall, $300-325.

IDEAL TOY CORPORATION, compo swivel head marked 13 SHIRLEY TEMPLE Copy IDEAL N&TCo.; mohair wig, glass-like sleep eyes, open mouth; compo jointed body marked SHIRLEY TEMPLE. Original condition in original trunk. 13″ tall, $75-100; trunk, $50-60.

IDEAL TOY CORPORATION, "MOR-TIMER SNERD" & BABY SNOOKS, compo swivel head; molded/painted hair, painted eyes, closed mouth; wood and "FLEXY" metal body with compo hands and wood feet. All original with tag. 12½" tall, **each $85-100.**

IDEAL TOY CORPORATION, "PIN-OCCHIO," compo swivel head marked CoP W. D.P. IDEAL DOLL; molded/painted hair, painted eyes, closed mouth; compo/wood jointed body with molded/painted clothes. 11" tall, $100-125.

IDEAL TOY CORPORATION, "SHIR-LEY TEMPLE," all compo, swivel head marked large "C"/OP inside IDEAL N & T CO.; mohair wig, plastic sleep eyes, open mouth; body jointed shoulders and hips. 18" tall, $125-150.

IDEAL TOY COMPANY, "FLOSSIE FLIRT," compo head marked U S IDEAL (in a diamond) OF A; saran wig, metal flirting sleep eyes, open mouth; cloth body with voice box, compo arms and legs. 20" tall, $100-125.

KNICKERBOKER TOY COMPANY, "DONALD DUCK," all molded/painted compo plus velvet cape and velour hat; body marked WALT DISNEY KNICKERBOKER TOY CO. All original. 10" tall, $125-150.

THREE-IN-ONE DOLL CORPORATION, "TRUDY," compo swivel head with three faces; wisps of mohair attached to hood, painted eyes, "sleepy, weepy, smiley" faces, cloth body. Original costume. 16″ tall, $100-125.

LEE, H. D., COMPANY, INC., all compo, jointed at shoulders, molded/painted hair, painted eyes, closed mouth. Label on pants reads Union Made LEE Reg. U. S. Pat. Off. 12½″ tall, $125-150.

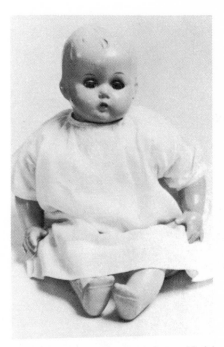

RELIABLE TOY COMPANY, compo swivel head; nylon wig, plastic sleep eyes, open mouth, compo jointed body. Label reads HER HIGHNESS CORONATION DOLL. All original. 15½″ tall, $65-80.

UNMARKED, all compo; molded/painted hair, features, shoes and socks; jointed at shoulders. 6″ tall, $30-40.

UNMARKED, compo head; molded/painted hair, metal sleep eyes, open/closed mouth; cloth body/compo arms and legs. 21″ long, 15″ head circumference, $65-80.

UNMARKED, "SHIRLEY TEMPLE,"
compo swivel head; mohair wig, glass-like sleep eyes, open mouth, compo jointed body. All original. 13" and 14" tall, each $100-125.

UNMARKED, SHIRLEY TEMPLE TODDLER, compo swivel head; human hair wig, glass-like sleep eyes, open mouth, compo jointed body. All original. 17" tall, $125-150.

UNMARKED, "SHIRLEY TEMPLE,"
compo swivel head; human hair (replacement) wig, glass-like sleep eyes, open mouth, compo jointed body. 20" tall, $100-125.

UNMARKED, compo swivel head; human hair wig, glass-like sleep eyes, closed mouth, compo jointed body. 26" tall, $100-125.

UNMARKED, "SHIRLEY TEMPLE,"
compo swivel head; mohair wig, metal sleep eyes, open mouth; compo jointed body. 17½" tall, $100-125.

UNMARKED, AMERICAN WAVE, all
compo, jointed at hips and shoulders;
molded/painted cap and hair, painted
eyes, closed mouth. Tag reads
W.A.V.E.S. All original. 14½" tall,
$65-90.

UNMARKED, AMERICAN SOLDIER,
all compo, jointed at hips and shoulders; molded/painted cap and hair,
painted eyes, closed mouth. Tag reads
Praise The Lord and Pass The Ammu-
nition. All original. 14½" tall, $65-90.

UNMARKED, compo swivel head; mohair wig, glass-like sleep eyes, open mouth, compo jointed body. 17½" tall, $75-100.

UNMARKED, compo swivel head; mohair wig, metal sleep eyes, open mouth, compo jointed body. All original. 19" tall, $75-100.

UNMARKED, all brown compo, jointed at hips and shoulders; molded/painted hair, painted eyes, closed mouth. 10" tall, $50-60.

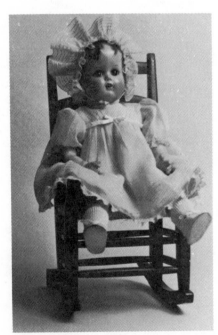

UNMARKED, compo flange head; molded/painted hair, glass-like sleep eyes, open mouth; cloth body with compo arms and legs. All original. 19½" tall, $65-85.

UNMARKED, compo flange head; molded/painted hair, glass-like sleep eyes, open mouth; cloth body with compo arms and legs. All original. 15" tall, $65-85.

UNMARKED, "SNOW WHITE & SEVEN DWARFS," all compo, jointed at hips and shoulders; molded/painted hair, painted eyes, closed mouth. Dwarfs, all molded/painted compo. Snow White, 13½" tall, $70-80; 8" dwarfs, each $40-50.

UNMARKED, all brown compo, jointed at hips and shoulders; molded/painted hair plus three yarn pigtails, painted eyes, closed mouth. 14" long, $90-100.

UNMARKED, all brown compo, jointed at hips and shoulders; molded/painted hair plus three yarn pigtails, painted eyes, closed mouth. 12" long, $75-85.

UNMARKED, LITTLE BO PEEP, compo swivel head; mohair wig, metal sleep eyes, closed mouth, compo jointed body. 14½" tall, $75-100.

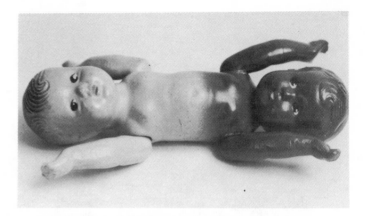

UNMARKED, TOPSY-TURVY DOLL, all compo, half brown-half white; molded/painted hair, painted eyes, closed mouth; both sets of arms jointed at shoulders. 7" long, $60-75.

WONDERCRAFT COMPANY, "BOBBIE MAE/SWING'N'SWAY," all compo, body and head swing side to side; molded/painted hair, painted eyes, closed mouth, molded/painted dress and bow. 11" tall, $90-100.

UNMARKED, COMIC CHARACTER, compo flange head; molded/painted hair, painted eyes, closed mouth; cloth body with compo hands. 13½" tall, $60-70.

UNMARKED, DIONNE QUINTUPLETS, all compo, jointed at hips and shoulders; molded/painted hair, painted eyes, closed mouth. 7½" long, **set** $75-100.

CRECHE DOLLS

TERRA COTTA shoulder head, molded/painted hair, inset glass eyes, closed mouth; hemp body with detailed wood hands and feet. All original. 20″ tall, $600-650.

TERRA COTTA shoulder head, molded/painted hair, glass inset eyes, closed mouth; hemp body with carved painted arms and legs (fine detail). 20″ tall, $725-750.

WOOD, CRECHE SET, all hand carved by "TITA LING," figures have carved/painted hair and beard, glass inset eyes with hair upper and lower lashes, closed mouth; Mary has human hair wig; carved/painted "treasures" and sandals; animals are carved/painted with painted eyes. All very fine detail. 3½″ tall to 11½″ tall, **14 pc. set $650-700.**

FOREIGN, in native costumes

Arranged alphabetically by country of origin

BERMUDA, brown velvet head, molded/painted features; brown velvet torso, arms and feet with stitched fingers and toes, velvet trousers, felt hat. All original. 7″ tall, $30-40.

CHINA, MERCHANT AND WIFE, mache head, molded/painted hair, painted eyes, closed mouth; straw stuffed paper body with mache hands and plaster feet. All original. 13½″ tall, **pair $350-400.**

CHINA, BOYS, mache head, painted eyes, closed mouth; cardboard body with mache arms and legs. 10″ tall, $100-125; 15½″ tall, $150-175.

CHINA, mache head; boy has painted hair with wisps of human hair; girl has molded/painted hair with ornate head piece; both have cloth bodies with mache hands. All original. 10″ tall, **each $150-200.**

CHINA, MONKEY KING, "Sixteenth Century Superman" in Chinese Opera; paper head with molded/painted features, ornate paper crown type hat; paper body with paper covered wire hands, plaster type molded/painted shoes, paper trouser legs; paper tag written in Chinese. All original. 9½" tall, rare, $225-250.

CHINA, ACTOR in Chinese Opera; plaster head, molded/painted features, ornate molded/painted paper head-dress, Chinese symbols on back of neck; paper covered straw-like wood torso with mache hands, wood/metal legs with painted wooden shoes. All original. 12" tall, $150-175.

CHINA, GENERAL KUAN YU, Actor in Chinese Opera, plaster type head, molded/painted ornate hat, long hair attached inside holes on each side of head, long beard inserted in slash above mouth, molded rust color painted face with painted features; paper covered straw-like wood body with mache hands, plaster type shoes; costume lined with paper printed in Chinese. All original. 10" tall, $175-200.

CHINA, ACTRESS; plaster type head, molded/painted hair with molded/painted ornate head dress; paper covered straw-like wood torso with mache hands, wood/metal legs and shoes (covered with cloth and braid). All original. 10" tall, $140-160.

CHINA, HUO MOH-LAN, Actress in Chinese Opera; plaster type head, molded/painted hair, features and hat with Chinese symbols painted on hat; paper covered straw-like wood body with mache hands and boots; rolled paper spear. All original. 10" tall, $150-175.

ENGLAND (?), KNIGHT in ARMOR, wood head, painted eyes, closed mouth; cloth body with woven metal armor. 8″ tall, $30-40.

ENGLAND, KING GEORGE V & QUEEN ELIZABETH II; all cloth, mohair wig, embroidered features. Tags read Liberty of London Dolls. 10″ tall, each $90-100.

ENGLAND, BOBBY, hard plastic head, molded/painted features, cloth body. Tag reads OLD COTTAGE DOLL. 10½″ tall, $30-40.

GREECE, cloth head, mohair wig, molded/painted features; unjointed hard plastic body. All original. 7½″ tall, $15-20.

GREECE, MAN, mache head, painted hair, painted eyes, closed mouth, all cloth body. 11½″ tall, $30-40.

GREECE, GIRL WEAVING; stationary head, silky fine thread type hair, cloth face with molded/painted features, plastic unjointed body. All original. 7″ tall, $15-20.

HAITI, BLACK WOMAN, all painted
wood, jointed at hips and shoulders.
9″ tall, $40-50.

HUNGARY, boy has mache head,
molded/painted hair and features;
girl has silky, fine, thread type hair,
molded/painted features; both have
all cloth bodies with stitched fingers;
oil-cloth shoes on boy, woolen shoes
on girl. All original. 9″ tall, **each**
$25-35.

IRELAND, NU-ART-DOLLS, marked
Georgene Novelties, Inc., U.S.A.; all
cloth, yarn type hair, molded/painted
features. All original. 14″ tall, **pair**
$45-55.

INDIA, DANCER; all cloth, thread
type hair, molded/painted features;
painted/stitched fingers and toes. All
original. 12″ tall, $40-50.

JAPAN, CRAWLING BABY, mache bobbing head, human hair wig, inset glass eyes, closed mouth; cardboard body with mache arms and legs. 8" long, $60-70.

ITALY, MUSICIAN; cloth head, silky thread-like hair, molded/painted features, hard plastic unjointed body. Original clothes with paper tag. 6" tall, $20-30.

ITALY, cloth head, fine thread type hair, molded/painted features; cloth body with plastic hands. All original. 8" tall, $20-30.

JAPAN, GEISHA GIRL, mache head, human hair wig, inset glass eyes, closed mouth; cloth/cardboard body with mache hands and feet. 8¼" tall, $25-35.

JAPAN, GIRL IN KIMONO, mache head, human hair wig, inset glass eyes, closed mouth; cardboard body with mache arms and legs. 14″ tall, $90-100.

JAPAN, SAMURAI WARRIORS, mache head, inset glass eyes, closed mouth; cloth body with wood hands and feet. 8½″ tall, **each $125-150.**

JAPAN, NOBILITY DOLLS, mache head, human hair wig, inset glass eyes, closed mouth; cardboard body with wood hands and feet. 3-5″ tall, **each $70-80.**

JAPAN, GIRL IN KIMONO, mache head, inset glass eyes, human hair wig, closed mouth; cardboard body with mache arms and legs. 24½″ tall, $120-130.

LATVIA, DANCERS, cloth head, floss and yarn hair, yarn face with embroidered features; cloth and wire body with crochet covered wire hands, crocheted clothes. All original. 7″ tall, **pair $110-120.**

NORWAY, GIRL, molded cloth head, hands, and feet; mohair wig, painted eyes, closed mouth; cloth body. 9″ tall, $25-35.

POLAND, all wood, yarn type hair, painted features. All original. 8″ tall, $10-20.

POLAND, celluloid head, silky fine, thread type hair; molded/painted features, all cloth body. All original. 14″ tall, $30-40.

RUSSIA, BOY & GIRL, mache head, mohair wig, painted eyes, closed mouth. 4″ tall, **each $20-30.**

RUSSIA, COSAQUE BOY & KAZAKH VILLAGE GIRL: all cloth, mohair wig, painted eyes, closed mouth. 7″ tall, **each $20-30.**

RUSSIA, all cloth; molded/painted features, string wrapped around legs, straw woven shoes. All original. 6″ tall, $25-35.

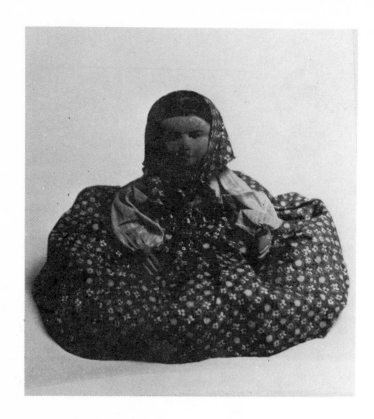

RUSSIA, TEA-COZY, stockinette head and hands, silky, thread type hair, molded/painted features; padded/quilted underskirt has cloth label, Made in Soviet Union—PEASANTS GIRL. All original. 6″ tall, $65-75.

RUSSIA, MALOWA WOMAN, all cloth, mohair wig, painted eyes, closed mouth. 15″ tall, $125-140.

RUSSIA, SMOLENSK DISTRICT WOMAN & VILLAGE BOY, all cloth; mohair wig, painted eyes, closed mouth. 15″ tall, each $125-140.

RUSSIA, WOMAN, mache head, mohair wig, painted eyes, closed mouth; cloth body with mache arms and legs. 14½″ tall, $125-150.

FRENCH BISQUE, babies

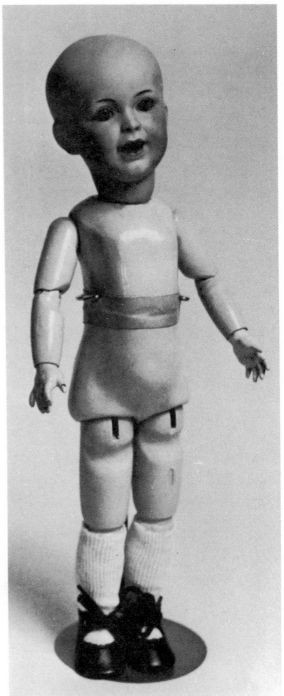

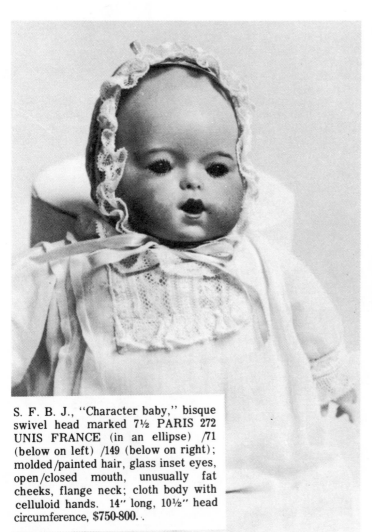

S. F. B. J., "Character baby," bisque swivel head marked 7½ PARIS 272 UNIS FRANCE (in an ellipse) /71 (below on left) /149 (below on right); molded/painted hair, glass inset eyes, open/closed mouth, unusually fat cheeks, flange neck; cloth body with celluloid hands. 14" long, 10½" head circumference, $750-800.

S. F. B. J., "Nursing—Character,"— bisque socket head marked S.F.B.J. 242 PARIS 6; bisque cap removable, very slightly molded/painted hair, glass inset eyes, open/closed mouth, round hole for nursing; mache/wood jointed body; hole between shoulder blades contains rubber tube which runs to the mouth. Rare. 17" tall, $2,200-2,500.

FRENCH BISQUE,

characters

*Arranged
by manufacturer*

LANTERNIER, A., & CIE, "TOTO," bisque socket, head marked DEOPSE TOTO N3 Mialono SC A L & C LIMOGES; human hair wig, paperweight eyes, open/closed mouth with two molded teeth and tongue, unusual expression; mache/wood jointed body. Rare. 16″ tall, $750-800.

S. F. B. J., "Character," bisque socket head marked S.F.B.J. 230 PARIS 10; human hair wig, glass inset eyes, open mouth; mache/wood jointed body. 22″ tall, $700-750.

S. F. B. J., "Character," bisque socket head marked S.F.B.J. 235 PARIS 8; molded/painted hair, glass inset eyes, open/closed mouth with two molded porcelain teeth; mache/wood jointed body. 18″ tall, $1,700-2,000.

S. F. B. J., "Character," bisque socket head marked UNIS FRANCE (in an ellipse), 71 (below on left) and 149 (below on right) 251 8; human hair wig, glass sleep eyes, open/closed mouth with two molded teeth and tongue; mache/wood jointed body. 17″ tall, $850-900.

S. F. B. J., "Character," TWIRP, bisque socket head marked FRANCE S.F.B.J. 247 PARIS 4; human hair wig, glass sleep eyes, open/closed mouth with two molded teeth and tongue; mache/wood jointed body. 14″ tall, $1,600-1,800.

S. F. B. J., "Character," bisque socket head marked x S.F.B.J. 236 PARIS -12-; human hair wig, glass sleep eyes, open/closed mouth with two molded teeth and tongue; mache/wood jointed body. 27" tall, $1,000-1,200.

S. F. B. J., "Character," bisque socket head marked S.F.B.J. 250 PARIS 11; human hair wig, glass sleep eyes, open mouth; mache/wood jointed body. Very rare! 25" tall, $2,500-2,700.

S. F. B. J., "Character," brown bisque socket head marked S.F.B.J. 227 PARIS 4; black slightly molded painted hair, glass inset eyes, open mouth with six molded porcelain teeth; brown mache/wood jointed body. 14" tall, $2,000-2,200.

S. F. B. J., "Character — Pouty," bisque socket head marked S.F.B.J. 252 PARIS 2; human hair wig, paperweight eyes, closed pouty mouth, frown creases on forehead and under eyes; mache/wood jointed body. 11½" tall, $2,500-2,700.

S. F. B. J., "Character," bisque socket head marked S.F.B.J. 226 PARIS 4; molded/painted hair, glass inset eyes, open/closed mouth with molded tongue; mache/wood jointed body. 13½" tall, $1,500-1,700.

FRENCH BISQUE, children

Arranged by manufacturer

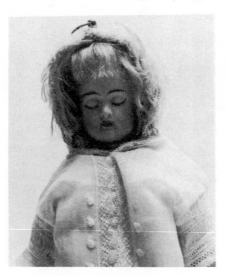

BRU, CASIMER(?), THREE FACE; brass knob/ring turns bisque head inside of a mache bonnet attached to a mache shoulder plate marked C B; mohair around bonnet front; smiling face has paperweight eyes, open/closed mouth; crying face has paperweight eyes, molded crystal tears, open/closed mouth; sleeping face has eyelids closed over eyes, closed mouth; cloth covered cardboard type torso, mache hands and legs. 11½" tall, $1,600-1,800.

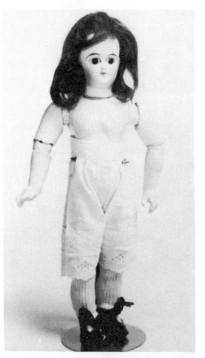

BRU (BRU JNE. & CIE), bisque socket head marked BRU Jne R 11; human
hair wig, paperweight eyes, open
mouth; mache/wood jointed body. 24"
tall, $2,200-2,500.

COMPANY UNIDENTIFIED, BEL-
TON TYPE, bisque socket head
marked unusual N or W over 2; mache/
wood jointed body. 10½" tall, $450-500.

BRU (BRU JNE. & CIE), bisque socket head marked BRU Jne 9; human
hair wig, paperweight eyes, closed
mouth; all kid body, bisque arms and
shoulder plate with molded breasts;
shoulder plate marked same as head.
23" tall, $5,700-6,000.

BRU (BRU JNE. & CIE), bisque socket head marked BRU Jne 7; human
hair wig, paperweight eyes, closed
mouth; kid/wood/metal articulated
body, bisque arms, shoulder plate
marked same as head. 17½" tall,
$5,200-5,500.

BRU (BRU JNE. & CIE), bisque socket head marked BREVETTE S.G.D.G.
BRU Jne R Y 10 M; original mohair
wig, paperweight eyes, closed mouth;
mache/wood jointed body marked
BEBE BRU N 10. 24" tall, $2,500-
2,700.

COMPANY UNIDENTIFIED, STEIN-ER, JULES NICHOLAS(?), OR CAY-ETTE, MADAM E.(?); bisque socket head marked five pointed star 90; human hair wig, paperweight eyes, open mouth; mache/wood jointed body. 19″ tall, $650-700.

COMPANY UNIDENTIFIED, bisque socket head marked M 3 B; human hair wig, paperweight eyes, closed mouth; mache/wood jointed body. 14″ tall, $1,100-1,300.

COMPANY NOT DEFINITELY IDENTIFIED, bisque socket head marked E11 D with red and black check marks; human hair wig, paperweight eyes, closed mouth; mache/wood jointed body. 24½″ tall, $1,400-1,600.

COMPANY UNIDENTIFIED, bisque socket head marked 10; human hair wig, glass sleep eyes, closed mouth; mache/wood jointed body (similar to Schmitt body). 14½″ tall, $650-700.

COMPANY UNIDENTIFIED, BEL-TON TYPE, bisque socket head marked 10 G F X; human hair wig, paperweight eyes, closed mouth; mache/wood jointed body. 14″ tall, $800-850.

COMPANY UNIDENTIFIED, bisque socket head marked 11; human hair wig, glass sleep eyes, closed mouth; mache/wood jointed body (similar to Schmitt body). 17″ tall, $850-900.

COMPANY UNIDENTIFIED, bisque socket head marked 16 79 DEP; human hair wig, glass paperweight sleep eyes, open mouth; mache/wood jointed body (similar to Schmitt body). 30″ tall, $750-800.

COMPANY UNIDENTIFIED, bisque socket head marked 183 12; human hair wig, paperweight eyes, closed mouth; mache/wood jointed body. 20″ tall, $1,200-1,400.

DANEL & CIE, bisque socket head marked PARIS BEBE TETE DEP 10; human hair wig, paperweight eyes, closed mouth; mache/wood jointed body. 25″ tall, $1,900-2,100.

FLEISCHMANN & BLODEL, bisque socket head marked EDEN BEBE PARIS 10 DEPOSE; human hair wig, paperweight eyes, open mouth; mache/wood jointed body. 23″ tall, $675-725.

GAULTIER (probably), bisque socket head marked F. G. inside scroll; human hair wig, paperweight eyes, closed mouth; mache/wood jointed body. 23″ tall, **$800-825.**

GAULTIER & FILS (probably), bisque socket head marked F6G; human hair wig, paperweight eyes, closed mouth; mache/wood jointed body. 15″ tall, **$625-675.**

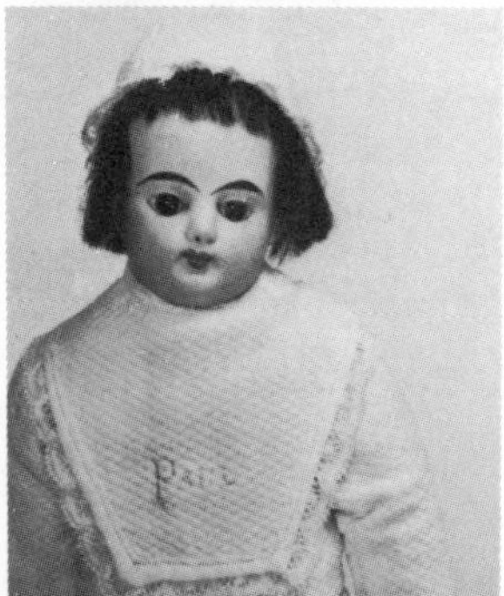

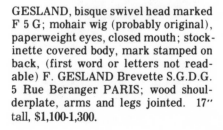

GAULTIER & FILS(?), BAPTEME OR CHRISTENING DOLL, bisque socket head marked F. G. (in a scroll) 6; human hair wig, paperweight eyes, closed mouth; mache torso and arms jointed at shoulders, bisque hands; mache lower portion container for sweetmeats. "Paul" ink stamped on bib. 12″ tall, **$700-750.**

GESLAND, bisque swivel head marked F 5 G; mohair wig (probably original), paperweight eyes, closed mouth; stockinette covered body, mark stamped on back, (first word or letters not readable) F. GESLAND Brevette S.G.D.G. 5 Rue Beranger PARIS; wood shoulderplate, arms and legs jointed. 17″ tall, **$1,100-1,300.**

JULLIEN, JR., bisque socket head marked JULLIEN 12; human hair wig, paperweight eyes, closed mouth; mache/wood jointed body. 30″ tall, $1,300-1,500.

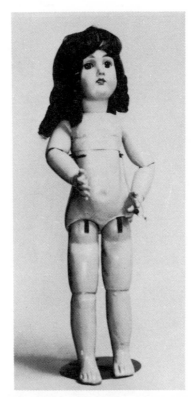

JUMEAU, bisque socket head marked DEPOSE TETE JUMEAU Bte S.G.D.-G. 15; human hair wig, paperweight eyes, closed mouth, applied pierced ears; mache/wood jointed body marked BEBE JUMEAU Diplome d'Honneur. 33″ tall, $1,400-1,600.

JULLIEN, JR., bisque socket head marked JULLIEN 8 importe; human hair wig, glass sleep eyes, open mouth; mache/wood jointed body marked with paper label, BEBE L'UNIVERSEL INCASSABLE; mama-papa pull cords. 23″ tall, $625-675.

JUMEAU, bisque socket head marked Depose TETE JUMEAU Bte SGDG; human hair wig, inset paperweight eyes, closed mouth; mache/wood jointed body marked JUMEAU MEDAILLE D'OR PARIS. 19½″ tall, $850-900.

JUMEAU, bisque socket head marked DEPOSE TETE JUMEAU Bte S.G.D.-G. 6 (red check marks); human hair wig, paperweight eyes, closed mouth; mache/wood jointed body marked JUMEAU MEDAILLE D'OR PARIS; mama-papa pull cords. 16″ tall, $875-925.

JUMEAU, bisque socket head marked
DEPOSE TETE JUMEAU Bte S.G.D.-
G. 6; (red check marks); human hair
wig, paperweight eyes, closed mouth;
mache/wood jointed body marked
BEBE JUMEAU Depose d'honneur.
15″ tall, $875-925.

JUMEAU, bisque socket head marked
DEPOSE TETE JUMEAU Bte S.G.D.-
G. 2 H8; human hair wig, paperweight
eyes, closed mouth; mache/wood
jointed body. 11″ tall, RARE SIZE,
$925-950.

JUMEAU, bisque socket head marked
Depose TETE JUMEAU Bte SGDG;
human hair wig, inset paperweight
eyes, closed mouth; mache/wood
jointed body marked JUMEAU MED-
AILLE D'OR PARIS. 18½″ tall,
$1,800-2,200.

JUMEAU, bisque socket head marked
1907 16; human hair wig, paperweight
eyes, open mouth; mache/wood jointed body. 33″ tall, $750-800.

JUMEAU, PORTRAIT, pale bisque
socket head, unmarked; human hair
wig, inset paperweight eyes, closed
mouth; mache/wood jointed body
marked JUMEAU MEDAILLE D'OR
PARIS. 16″ tall, $925-950.

JUMEAU, bisque socket head marked
DEPOSE TETE JUMEAU Bte S.G.D.-
G. 11; human hair wig, paperweight
eyes, closed mouth, applied pierced
ears; mache/wood jointed body
marked BEBE JUMEAU Diplome
d'Honneur. In original box. 24″ tall,
$950-1,000.

JUMEAU, bisque socket head marked
DEPOSE TETE JUMEAU Bte S.G.D.-
G. 11 (red check marks); human hair
wig, paperweight eyes, closed mouth;
mache/wood jointed body marked
JUMEAU MEDAILLE D'OR DE-
POSE. Original dress in original box.
23″ tall, $950-1,000.

JUMEAU, bisque socket head marked
DEPOSE TETE JUMEAU Bte SGDG;
human hair wig, inset paperweight
eyes, closed mouth; mache/wood
jointed body marked JUMEAU MED-
AILLE D'OR PARIS. 16″ tall, $1,800-
2,000.

JUMEAU, bisque socket head marked DEPOSE TETE JUMEAU Bte S.G.D.-G. 10 H H I; human hair wig, paperweight eyes, closed mouth; mache/wood jointed body marked BEBE JUMEAU HORS CONCOURS DEPOSE. 22" tall, $950-1,000.

JUMEAU, EMILE, "Portrait Jumeau," bisque socket head marked J; human hair wig, paperweight eyes, closed mouth; mache/wood jointed body. 17" tall, $950-1,000.

JUMEAU, EMILE, "LONG FACE," bisque socket head marked 12; human hair wig, paperweight eyes, closed mouth, applied pierced ears; mache/wood jointed body marked JUMEAU MEDAILLE D'OR PARIS. 25½" tall, $4,500-4,800.

JUMEAU, bisque socket head marked DEPOSE TETE JUMEAU Bte S.G.D.-G. 12 A X 1; human hair wig, paperweight eyes, closed mouth, applied pierced ears; mache/wood jointed body marked JUMEAU MEDAILLE D'OR PARIS, "CLINIQUE DES POUPEES SPte DES BEBES CARTIER 6 RUE MONTORGE GRENOBLE" (on paper label); mama-papa pull cords. 27" tall, $1,450-1,600.

JUMEAU, bisque socket head marked DEPOSE TETE JUMEAU Bte S.G.D.-G. 13 v x; human hair wig, paperweight eyes, closed mouth, applied pierced ears; mache/wood jointed body marked BEBE JUMEAU MEDAILLE D'OR PARIS, 28" tall, $1,400-1,600.

JUMEAU, bisque socket head marked TETE JUMEAU 8; human hair wig, paperweight eyes, open mouth; mache/wood jointed body marked BEBE JUMEAU Diplome d'Honneur; mama-papa pull cords, walking mechanism. 17" tall, $650-700.

JUMEAU(?), "Walker-kisser," bisque socket head marked 8; human hair wig, paperweight eyes, open mouth; mache/wood jointed body. 21" tall, $625-650.

LANTERNIER, A., & CIE, bisque socket head marked MON CHERIE L. G. PARIS 6; human hair wig, paperweight eyes, open/closed mouth with molded porcelain teeth; mache/wood jointed body, mama pull cord. 16½" tall, $625-650.

RABERY & DELPHIEU, bisque socket head marked R 4 D.; human hair wig, paperweight eyes, closed mouth; mache/wood jointed body. 28½" tall, $950-1,000.

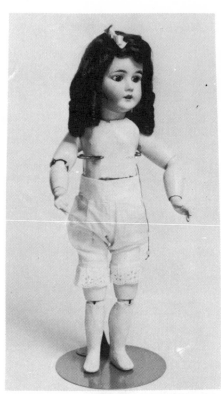

ROSTAL, M. (HENRY), bisque socket head marked 295 MON TRESOR 9; human hair wig, paperweight eyes, open mouth; mache/wood jointed body, mama-papa pull cords. 22" tall, $725-750.

SCHMITT & FILS (SONS), bisque socket head marked with crossed hammers over SCH inside of a shield; human hair wig, paperweight eyes, closed mouth; mache/wood jointed body; mark on torso bottom same as head. 14" tall, RARE, $2,500-2,700.

S. F. B J., painted plaster-bisque socket head marked S F B J PARIS 3 /0; mohair wig, glass sleep eyes, closed mouth; mache jointed body; tag reads Made in Martinique. 12½" tall, $225-250.

S. F. B. J., bisque socket head marked S.F.B.J. PARIS 3 (Jumeau mold); human hair wig, paperweight eyes, open mouth; mache /wood jointed body. 20" tall, $600-650.

S. F. B. J., brown bisque socket head marked UNIS FRANCE (in an oval) 60 12 /0; mohair wig, inset glass pupil-less eyes, open mouth; mache jointed body. 10½" tall, $250-275.

S. F. B. J., bisque socket head marked S F B J 60 PARIS 13 /0; mohair wig, inset glass pupil-less eyes, closed mouth; mache jointed body. 8" tall, $150-175.

STEINER, JULES NICHOLAS, bisque socket head marked J. STEINER Bte S.G.D.G. PARIS F.I.re A 7; human hair wig, paperweight eyes, closed mouth; all-metal jointed body. 15½" tall, $1,500-1,700.

STEINER, JULES NICHOLAS, BEBE STEINER, bisque socket head marked J. STEINER Bte S.G.D.G. PARIS FIre, A 7; human hair wig, paper-weight eyes, closed mouth; mache/ wood jointed body marked LE PETIT PARISIEN BEBE J. STEINER MARQUE DEPOSE MEDAILLE D'OR PARIS 1889 (paper label). 15" tall, $1,300-1,500.

STEINER, JULES NICHOLAS, bisque socket head marked J. STEINER Bte S.G.D.G. F.I.re A 13; human hair wig, paperweight eyes, closed mouth; mache/wood jointed body. 20½" tall, $1,500-1,700.

STEINER, JULES NICHOLAS, "PHE-NIX," bisque socket head marked five pointed star 92; human hair wig, paperweight eyes, closed mouth; mache/wood jointed body; mama-papa pull cords. 22" tall, $1,800-2,000.

TIBUREE, ALEXANDRE CELESTIN, "BEBE MOTHEREAU," bisque socket head marked B. M.; human hair wig, paperweight eyes, closed mouth; mache/wood jointed body. 23" tall, $1,900-2,100.

STEINER, JULES NICHOLAS, bisque socket head marked STEINER Bte S.G.D.G. Sie C 3 BOURGOIN Jne; human hair wig, wire handle at crown of head behind ear opens and closes the glass eyes, closed mouth; mache/wood jointed body. 20" tall, $1,900-2,200.

UNMARKED, BRU TYPE, bisque swivel head on bisque shoulder plate; mohair wig, glass sleep eyes, open/closed mouth with five molded teeth; kid body with bisque arms. 19½" tall, $1,900-2,200.

FRENCH BISQUE,

fashions

*Arranged
by manufacturer*

GAULTIER (probably), FRENCH FASHION, bisque swivel head; mohair wig, paperweight eyes, closed mouth; bisque shoulder plate marked F. G.; kid gusseted adult body with individually wired and stitched fingers. 12½″ tall, $800-850.

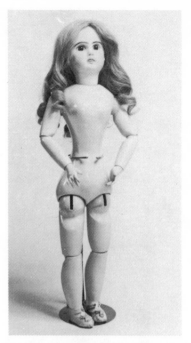

JUMEAU, bisque socket head marked X over 7; human hair wig, paperweight eyes, open mouth; mache/wood jointed adult body marked BEBE JUMEAU Diplome d'Honneur. 220 tall, $700-750.

UNMARKED, FRENCH FASHION, bisque socket head; human hair wig, paperweight eyes, closed mouth; adult kid body, fingers individually wired and stitched, bisque shoulder plate. 33″ tall, $2,600-2,800.

ROHMER, untinted parian type bisque swivel head; mohair wig, paperweight eyes, closed mouth; bisque shoulder plate and arms; kid/wood body and legs, marked on stomach MME ROHMER BREVETE S.G.D.G. PARIS (in an oval); typical two eyelet holes below the mark, jointed shoulders and hips. 16″ tall, $2,850-3,000.

UNMARKED, FRENCH FASHION, parian quality bisque shoulder head; mohair wig, paperweight eyes, closed mouth, head bent forward looking down; kid body, individually wired and stitched fingers. 15″ tall, $750-800.

UNMARKED, FRENCH FASHION, bisque swivel head on bisque shoulder plate; mohair wig, inset glass eyes, closed mouth; kid adult body with bisque arms. 17½″ tall, $800-850.

UNMARKED, YOUNG GIRL FASH-ION, bisque swivel head on bisque shoulder plate; mohair wig, inset glass eyes, closed mouth; kid adult body with bisque arms. 15″ tall, $475-500.

UNMARKED, FRENCH FASHION, bisque swivel head on bisque shoulder plate; mohair wig, inset glass eyes, closed mouth; kid adult body with individually stitched and wired fingers. 11½″ tall, $650-700.

UNMARKED, SMILING FASHION, bisque swivel head on bisque shoulder plate; mohair wig, inset glass eyes, closed smiling mouth; kid adult body with individually stitched fingers. 16″ tall, $900-950.

113

GERMAN BISQUE, babies

Arranged
by manufacturer

ALT, BECK & GOTTSCHALCK(?), "Character," bisque socket head marked A. B. & G. 1322 over 55; human hair wig, glass sleep eyes, open mouth; mache/wood jointed baby body. 22" long, 17" head circumference, $475-500.

AVERILL, MADAME GEORGENE, "Character," bisque swivel head marked GEORGENE AVERILL 1005 3652 Germany; molded/painted hair, glass sleep eyes, open mouth, flange neck; cloth body with compo arms and legs. 22" long, 14½" head circumference, $775-800.

AVERILL, MADAME GEORGENE, "Character," bisque flange head marked, copy. by Georgene Averill 1005/3652 Germany; painted hair, glass sleep eyes, open mouth; cloth body with compo arms and legs. 15" long, 11½" head circumference, $700-750.

114

BAHR & PROSCHILD, bisque socket head marked 604 (over) 5; mohair wig, glass sleep eyes, open mouth; mache jointed baby body. 13″ long, 11″ head circumference, $250-300.

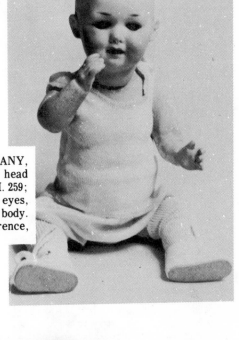

BORGFELDT, GEO., & COMPANY, "Character," bisque socket head marked G 326 B A 3 M D.R.G.M. 259; molded/painted hair, glass sleep eyes, open mouth; mache jointed baby body. 14″ long, 9½″ head circumference, $250-300.

COMPANY UNIDENTIFIED, "Character," breather baby, bisque socket head marked Made in Germany 100/12; human hair wig, glass sleep eyes, open nostrils, open mouth, oscillating tongue; mache/wood jointed baby body. 23″ long, 15″ head circumference, $475-500.

GANS, OTTO, bisque socket head marked OTTO GANS Germany 975 A. 11. M.; human hair wig, glass sleep eyes, open mouth; mache/wood jointed baby body. 22″ long, 14″ head circumference, $350-400.

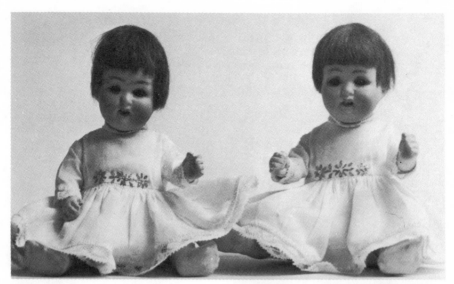

HEUBACH, ERNST, bisque socket
head marked Heubach Kopplesdorf
300 19/0 Germany; mohair wig, glass
sleep eyes, open mouth; mache jointed
baby body. 7" long, 5½" head circumference, each $150-175.

HEUBACH, ERNST, "Character,"
bisque socket head marked HEU-
BACH-KOPPELSDORF 300 · 3 Germany; human hair wig, glass sleep
eyes, open mouth; mache/wood jointed baby body. 18" long, 13" head circumference, $350-400.

HEUBACH, ERNST, "Character,"
bisque socket head marked HEU-
BACH-KOPPELSDORF 300 · 7/0 Germany; human hair wig, glass sleep
eyes, open mouth; mache/wood jointed baby body. 12½" long, 9½" head
circumference, $250-300.

116

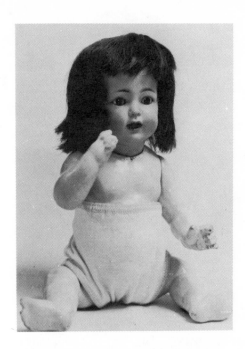

HEUBACH, ERNST, "Character," bisque socket head marked Heubach Kopplesdorf 320-2 Germany; mohair wig, glass sleep eyes, open mouth, open nostrils; mache jointed baby body. 19″ long, 13″ head circumference, $275-300.

KAMMER & REINHARDT, bisque socket head marked K STAR R S & H 122 32; human hair wig, glass sleep eyes, open mouth; mache/wood jointed baby body. 13½″ long, 10″ head circumference, $275-300.

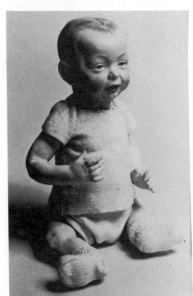

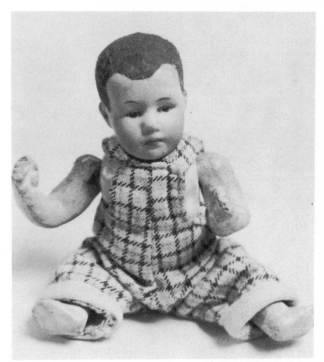

KAMMER & REINHARDT, BABY, "Character," bisque socket head marked K STAR R 100 50; molded/painted hair, painted eyes, open/closed mouth; mache/wood jointed baby body. 19″ long, 14″ head circumference, $775-800.

HEUBACH, GEBRUDER, bisque socket head marked (sun w/rays) G. H. Germany; flocked hair, molded/painted intaglio eyes, closed mouth; jointed mache baby body. 6″ long, 4½″ head circumference, $225-250.

117

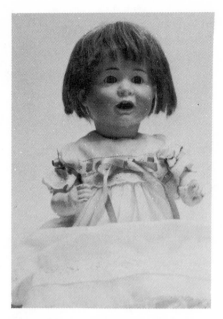

KAMMER & REINHARDT, "Character," bisque socket head marked K STAR R SIMON & HALBIG S & H 126 56; human hair wig, glass sleep eyes, open mouth; mache/wood jointed baby body. 26″ long, 17″ head circumference, $550-600.

KAMMER & REINHARDT, "Character Baby," bisque socket head marked K STAR R SIMON & HALBIG 116 A 42; human hair wig, glass sleep eyes, open mouth; mache/wood jointed baby body. 14″ long, 12½″ head circumference, $600-650.

KESTNER, J. D., JR., bisque shoulder head marked J.D.K. 235; human hair wig, glass sleep eyes, open mouth; kid body marked (paper label) crown and streamers-J.D.K. Germany; one-half cork stuffed, compo arms and legs. 11½″ long, 9″ head circumference, $400-450.

KESTNER, J. D., JR., "Character," bisque socket head marked Made in F. Germany 10 211 J.D.K.; mohair wig, glass sleep eyes, open mouth; mache/ wood jointed baby body. 12½″ long, 10″ head circumference, $350-375.

KESTNER, J. D., Jr., "Character," bisque socket head marked J. D. K. Made in 14 Germany; painted hair, glass sleep eyes, open mouth; mache jointed baby body. 16″ long, 13½″ head circumference, $375-400.

KESTNER, J. D., JR., "Character," bisque socket head marked Made in Germany 152 3; mohair wig, glass sleep eyes, open mouth; mache/wood jointed baby body. 12″ long, 9″ head circumference, $325-350.

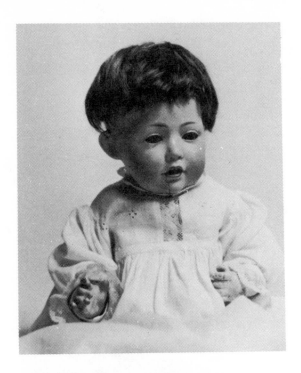

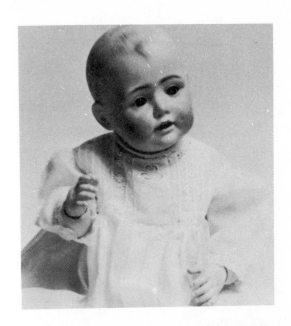

KESTNER, J. D., JR., "Character,"
bisque socket head marked J. D. K.
Made in 17 Germany; molded/painted
hair, glass sleep eyes, open mouth;
mache/wood jointed baby body. 22"
long, 16" head circumference, $525-550.

KESTNER, J. D., JR., HILDA, "Character," bisque socket head marked
Made in F Germany 10 237 J D K Jr.
1914 c (in circle) Hilda Gesgesh N.
1070; mohair wig, glass sleep eyes,
open mouth; mache/wood jointed baby
body. 12" long, 10" head circumference, $700-750.

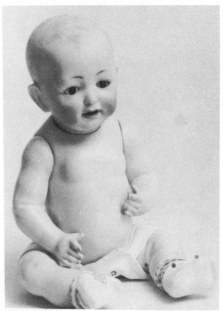

KESTNER, J. D., Jr., "Character,"
bisque socket head marked J. D. K.
Made in Germany; painted hair, glass
sleep eyes, open mouth; mache jointed
baby body. 14½" long, 11" head circumference, $300-350.

KESTNER, J. D., Jr., "Character,"
bisque socket head marked Made in
Germany 152 4; mohair wig, glass
sleep eyes, open mouth; mache jointed
baby body. 12" long, 10" head circumference, $275-300.

119

MARSEILLE, ARMAND, bisque flange head marked A. M. Germany 347-19; painted hair, glass sleep eyes, closed mouth; cloth body with bisque (replacement) hands. 13" long, 9" head circumference, $175-200.

KLEY & HAHN, "Character," bisque socket head marked K & H (in a streamer) Germany 167-15; human hair wig, glass sleep eyes, open mouth; mache/wood jointed baby body. 26" long, 17" head circumference, $500-600.

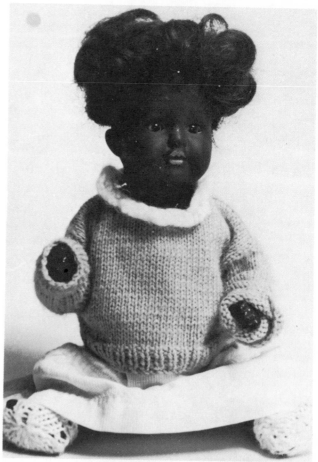

MARSEILLE, ARMAND, bisque socket head marked Germany 341/3K. A.M.; painted hair, glass sleep eyes, closed mouth; mache jointed baby body. 9" long, 7½" head circumference, $225-250.

MARSEILLE, ARMAND, brown bisque socket head marked ARMAND MARSEILLE Germany 990 A 7/0 M; human hair wig, glass sleep eyes, open mouth; brown mache/wood jointed baby body. 11" long, 7½" head circumference, $275-300.

MARSEILLE, ARMAND, CRYING DREAM BABY, bisque swivel head marked A M Germany 347/3; molded/painted hair, glass sleep eyes, open/closed mouth, cloth body, compo hands. 12″ long, 10½″ head circumference, $325-350.

MARSEILLE, ARMAND, ORIENTAL, olive color bisque socket head marked A ELLAR (in a star) M Germany 4.K; painted hair, glass sleep eyes, closed mouth; olive color mache jointed baby body. 14½″ long, 12½″ head circumference, $500-550.

MARSEILLE, ARMAND, ORIENTAL, light olive bisque socket head marked A. M. Germany 353/3 K.; molded/painted hair, glass sleep eyes, closed mouth; mache/wood jointed baby body. 12″ long, 10″ head circumference, $550-575.

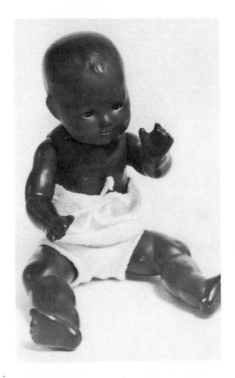

MARSEILLE, ARMAND, ROCKABY, brown painted bisque head marked A. M. Germany 351/1 K.; molded/painted hair, glass sleep eyes, open mouth; brown mache/wood jointed baby body. 13″ long, 10″ head circumference, $350-400.

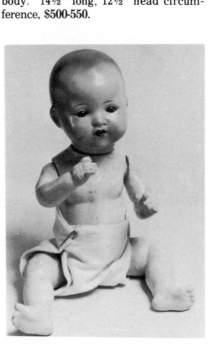

MARSEILLE, ARMAND, ROCKABY, painted bisque socket head marked A. M. Germany 351/3¼ K; molded/painted hair, glass sleep eyes, open mouth; mache jointed baby body. 14½″ long, 12½″ head circumference, $325-350.

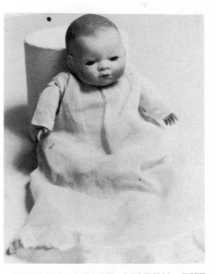

PUTNAM, GRACE STOREY, BYE-LO, bisque swivel head marked Copr. BY GRACE S. PUTNAM MADE IN GERMANY; molded/painted hair, glass sleep eyes, closed mouth, flange neck; cloth body, red ink stamped BYE - LO - BABY Pat. Appl'd For, COPY BY GRACE STOREY PUTNAM; celluloid hands. 11″ long, 10″ head circumference, $400-450.

PUTNAM, GRACE STOREY, BYE-LO, bisque swivel head marked Copr. BY GRACE S. PUTNAM MADE IN GERMANY; molded/painted hair, glass sleep eyes, closed mouth, flange neck; cloth body, stamped red ink, BYE - LO - BABY Pat. Appl'd For COPY BY GRACE STOREY PUTNAM; celluloid hands. 14″ long, 12½″ head circumference, **$475-500.**

PUTNAM, GRACE STOREY, BYE-LO, bisque swivel head marked Copr. BY GRACE S. PUTNAM MADE IN GERMANY; slightly molded/painted hair, glass sleep eyes, closed mouth, flange neck; cloth body, marked red ink, BYE-LO-BABY PAT. APPL'D FOR COPY BY GRACE STOREY PUTNAM; celluloid hands. 21″ long, 17″ head circumference, **$750-800.**

RECKNAGEL, TH., bisque socket head marked Germany 3½ R. 138 A.; molded/painted hair, glass sleep eyes, closed mouth; mache jointed baby body. 14″ long, 11″ head circumference, **$325-350.**

REINECKE, OTTO, "Character," bisque socket head marked P. M. 23 Germany 4½; mohair wig, glass sleep eyes, open mouth; mache jointed baby body. 15″ long, 11½″ head circumference, **$200-225.**

REINECKE, OTTO, GRETE, "Character," bisque socket head marked P. M. Grete 2; mohair wig, glass sleep eyes, open mouth; mache/wood jointed baby body. 15½″ long, 11″ head circumference, **$250-300.**

UNMARKED, "Character," bisque socket head; painted hair, painted intaglio eyes, open/closed mouth; mache jointed baby body. 13″ long, 9″ head circumference, $200-225.

SCHMIDT, FRANZ, & COMPANY, "Character," bisque socket head marked F.S. & Co. (large) X SIMON & HALBIG 1397 made in Germany 52; mohair wig, glass sleep eyes, open mouth; mache/wood jointed baby body. 20″ long, 15″ head circumference, $450-500.

WOLF, LOUIS & COMPANY, "Character," bisque socket head marked 152 L. W. & Co. (in a square) 7; mohair wig, glass sleep eyes, open mouth; mache jointed baby body. 15″ long, 12″ head circumference, $225-250.

WOLF, LOUIS & COMPANY, "Character," bisque socket head marked 152 (over) 7; mohair wig, glass sleep eyes, open mouth; mache jointed baby body, 16″ long, 12½″ head circumference, $240-260.

WOLF, LOUIS & COMPANY, "Character," bisque socket head marked 152 (over) 6; mohair wig, glass sleep eyes, open mouth; mache jointed baby body. 14″ long, 11″ head circumference, $225-250.

GERMAN BISQUE, characters

Arranged

by manufacturer

HEUBACH, GEBRUDER, bisque socket head marked 8192 Germany Gebruder Heubach (sun rays mark) G 2/0 ½ H; mohair wig, glass sleep eyes, open mouth. 14″ tall, $425-450.

BAHR & PROCHILD, "Character," bisque socket head marked 678 B P (in a heart) made in Germany; human hair wig, glass sleep eyes, open mouth; mache/wood jointed body. 19″ tall, $250-300.

HEUBACH, GEBRUDER, bisque socket head marked 28 4/0; white molded cap with blue tassel, painted intaglio eyes, open/closed mouth with two molded teeth; mache jointed body. 10½″ tall, $500-550.

HEUBACH, GEBRUDER, bisque socket head marked 8192 Germany Gebruder Heubach G 1 H; mohair wig, glass sleep eyes, open mouth; mache/wood jointed body. 14½″ tall, $425-450.

124

HEUBACH, GEBRUDER, bisque socket head marked 76 3 02 (GH sun segment mark) Germany; flocked hair, painted intaglio eyes, closed pouty mouth; mache jointed body. 12½″ tall, $525-550.

HEUBACH, GEBRUDER, bisque socket head marked 8420 5 HEUBACH (in a square) Germany; mohair wig, glass sleep eyes, closed pouty mouth; mache/wood jointed body. 15″ tall, $300-350.

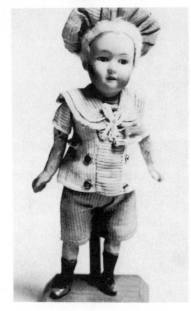

HEUBACH, GEBRUDER, bisque socket head marked 8192 Germany Gebruder Heubach HEU over BACH (in a square) G 14 over 4 H; mohair wig, painted intaglio eyes, closed mouth; mache body, jointed shoulders and hips, painted shoes and socks. Clothes all original. 7½″ tall, $225-250.

HEUBACH, GEBRUDER, bisque shoulder head marked 2/0 D 85 47 HEUBACH (in a square) Germany; molded/painted hair, painted intaglio eyes, closed pouty mouth; kid body with bisque arms. 12½" tall, $550-575.

HEUBACH, GEBRUDER, (left) bisque socket head marked Germany; molded/painted hair, painted intaglio eyes, closed mouth, mache/wood jointed body; (right) same except head marked 4 Germany, open/closed mouth with two molded teeth. 14½" tall (left), $500-550. 15" tall (right), $500-550.

HEUBACH, GEBRUDER, "Whistling Jim," bisque flange head marked 5 57 74 HEUBACH (in a square) Germany; molded/painted hair, painted intaglio eyes, open whistling mouth; cloth, excelsior stuffed body with compo arms, squeaker in torso. 13½" tall, $600-650.

KAMMER & REINHART, bisque socket head marked 11 K(star)R SIMON HALBIG 115/A; mohair wig, glass sleep eyes, closed, pouty mouth; mache/wood jointed body. 12½" tall, $750-800.

JAGER & COMPANY, "Pouty," bisque socket head marked F 3; flocked hair, glass inset eyes, closed pouty mouth; mache jointed body. 12½" tall, $800-825.

KAMMER & REINHART, "Character-Pouty," bisque socket head marked K star R 114 46; human hair wig, painted eyes, closed, pouty mouth; mache/wood jointed body. 18" tall, $2,200-2,400.

KOENIG & WERNICHE, "Character," bisque socket head marked K. & W. 9; mohair wig, glass sleep eyes, open mouth; mache/wood jointed body marked K. & W. made in Germany (inside a circle). 20" tall, $425-450.

KAMMER & REINHARDT, "Pouty,"
bisque socket head marked K STAR R
30 101 1909; human hair wig, painted
eyes, closed mouth, pouty expression;
mache/wood jointed body. 12" tall,
$875-900.

KESTNER, J. D., Jr., bisque socket
head marked K½ made in Germany
14½ 143; mohair wig, glass sleep eyes,
open mouth; mache/wood jointed
body. 29" tall, $425-450.

KESTNER, J. D., Jr., bisque socket
head marked J D K 260; mohair wig,
glass sleep eyes, open mouth; mache/
wood jointed body. 19½" tall, $350-
400.

KESTNER, J. D., JR., "Character," bisque socket head marked 14 Germany K; mohair wig, glass sleep eyes, open mouth; mache/wood jointed body. 22" tall, $425-450.

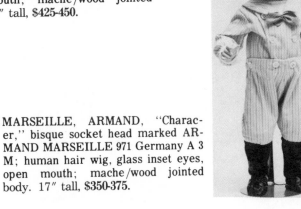

MARSEILLE, ARMAND, "Character," bisque socket head marked ARMAND MARSEILLE 971 Germany A 3 M; human hair wig, glass inset eyes, open mouth; mache/wood jointed body. 17" tall, $350-375.

MARSEILLE, ARMAND, painted bisque socket head marked Just Me Registered Germany A 310 7/0 M; mohair wig, glass googlie sleep eyes, closed mouth; jointed compo body. All original. 7½" tall, $300-325.

MARSEILLE, ARMAND, bisque socket head marked 323 Germany A 11/0 M; lamb's wool wig, glass googlie sleep eyes, closed mouth; mache jointed body. 7" tall, $300-350.

129

MARSEILLE, ARMAND, "Googlie," bisque socket head marked 258 A 3/0 M; human hair wig, glass inset googlie eyes, watermelon type mouth; mache/ wood jointed body. 12″ tall, $800-850.

MARSEILLE, ARMAND, "Just me," "Character," bisque socket head marked JUST ME Registered Germany A 310/10/0 M; mohair wig, glass sleep eyes glancing to side, pursed mouth; mache body jointed shoulders and hips. 7¾″ tall, $325-350.

SIMON & HALBIG, bisque socket head marked S 7 H 949; human hair wig, inset glass eyes, closed mouth; mache/ wood jointed body. 15½″ tall, $450-500.

MARSEILLE, ARMAND, "Nobbi Kids, Googlies," bisque socket head marked A 233 M NOBBI KIDS Reg. U. S. Pat. Off. Germany 11/0; human hair wig, glass googlie sleep eyes, closed mouth; mache body jointed shoulders and hips, molded/painted shoes and socks. 7¼″ tall, each $750-800.

SEYFARTH & REINHARDT, "Character," bisque socket head marked 989 SuR (over sun segment inside of a circle) 6 Germany (head made by Ernst Heubach); human hair wig, glass "flirting" sleep eyes, open mouth; mache/wood jointed body, voice box. 19″ tall, $425-450.

SIMON & HALBIG, bisque socket head marked S 9 H 949; human hair wig, inset glass eyes, closed pouty mouth; mache/wood jointed body. 16½" tall, $500-550.

SIMON & HALBIG, "Character," bisque socket head marked S 13 H 719 DEP; solid dome, human hair wig, glass inset eyes, closed mouth; mache/ wood jointed body. 22" tall, $750-800.

UNMARKED, bisque socket head; molded/painted hair, painted googlie eyes, closed mouth; mache body jointed at hips and shoulders with painted/ molded shoes and socks. 6½" tall, $275-300.

131

GERMAN BISQUE, children

Arranged
by manufacturer

COMPANY UNIDENTIFIED, "American School Boy," bisque shoulder head marked Germany 30 /35; molded /painted hair, inset glass eyes, closed mouth; kid body with bisque arms. 16" tall, $400-450.

BORGFELDT, GEO., & COMPANY (?), bisque socket head marked Germany G. B.; human hair wig, glass inset eyes, open mouth; mache /wood jointed body. 24" tall, $200-250.

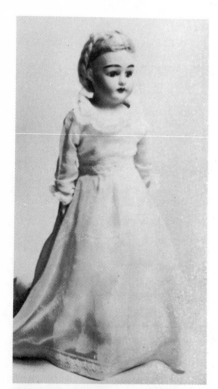

BORGFELDT, GEO., & COMPANY, "ALMA," bisque shoulder head marked ALMA 8/0; human hair wig, glass inset eyes, open mouth; kid gusseted body /bisque hands. 16" tall, $250-300.

BORGFELDT, GEO., & COMPANY, "PANSY," bisque socket head marked PANSY 1 Germany; human hair wig, glass inset eyes, open mouth; mache / wood jointed body. 24" tall, $300-350.

COMPANY UNIDENTIFIED "Patsy"(?), bisque swivel shoulder head marked Made in Germany; molded/painted hair, glass sleep eyes, open mouth; composition (Patsy type), jointed body. 18½" tall, $200-225.

COMPANY UNIDENTIFIED, bisque
shoulder head marked 3-0; human hair
wig, inset glass eyes, open mouth; kid
body with bisque arms. 13″ tall,
$150-175.

COMPANY UNIDENTIFIED, bisque
socket head marked 15; mohair wig,
glass inset eyes, closed mouth; mache
body jointed shoulders and hips, painted shoes. 5½″ tall, $125-150.

COMPANY UNIDENTIFIED, bisque
shoulder head marked 1235 Germany
N 9 DEP; human hair wig, inset glass
eyes, open mouth; kid body with bisque
arms. 21″ tall, $300-350.

COMPANY UNIDENTIFIED, bisque
head marked 3/0; yarn-like wigs, mold-
ed/painted features; wrapped yarn
bodies. 2½″ tall, set of six $200-240.

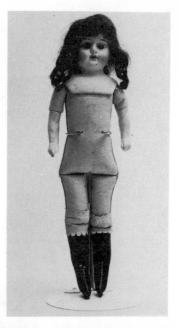

COMPANY UNIDENTIFIED, bisque shoulder head marked 3 148 Germany; human hair wig, inset glass eyes, open mouth; kid body with bisque arms. 15″ tall, $225-250.

COMPANY UNIDENTIFIED, bisque socket head marked Made in Germany; mohair wig, glass sleep eyes, open mouth; mache jointed body. 7½″ tall, $125-150.

COMPANY UNIDENTIFIED, bisque shoulder head marked 15/0; mohair wig, inset pupil-less glass eyes, open mouth; pink cloth body marked Made in Germany; mache arms and sewed on oilcloth shoes. 13″ tall, $110-130.

COMPANY UNIDENTIFIED, bisque shoulder head marked 11½ 115 135; human hair wig, glass sleep eyes, open mouth; kid body with bisque arms. 18″ tall, $175-200.

COMPANY UNIDENTIFIED, bisque socket head marked Germany; lambs wool wig, inset glass eyes, open mouth; mache jointed body. 12″ tall, $150-175.

GOEBEL, WILLIAM, bisque socket head marked "W. G" (intertwined) 120 3 Germany (in a rectangle); human hair wig, glass sleep eyes, open mouth; mache/wood jointed body. 16" tall, $175-200.

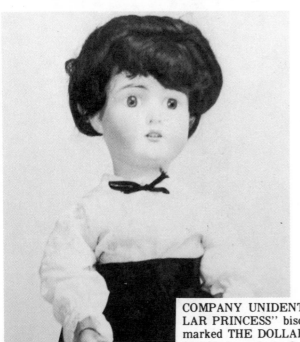

COMPANY UNIDENTIFIED, "DOLLAR PRINCESS" bisque socket head marked THE DOLLAR PRINCESS 62 SPECIAL made in Germany; mohair wig, glass sleep eyes, open mouth; mache/wood jointed body. 25" tall, $225-250.

HANDWERK, HEINRICH, bisque socket head marked 109-11 Germany Handwerk 2½; mohair wig, glass sleep eyes, open mouth; mache/wood jointed body. Original costume. 21" tall, $250-275.

HANDWERCK, MAX, bisque socket head marked 30 H (K over 3 inside the H); human hair wig, glass inset eyes, open mouth; mache/wood jointed body. 24½″ tall, $225-250.

HANDWERCK, HEINRICH, bisque socket head marked 11½ 99 DEP HANDWERCK 3; human hair wig, glass sleep eyes, open mouth; mache/ wood jointed body. 21″ tall, $250-300.

HANDWERCK, HEINRICH, bisque shoulder head marked Hch 3/0 H. Germany; human hair wig, glass inset eyes, open mouth; kid body with bisque arms. 19″ tall, $200-225.

HEUBACH, ERNST, bisque shoulder head marked Heubach 275 6 /0 Koppelsdorf Germany; human hair wig, glass sleep eyes, open mouth; kid body with bisque arms. 19″ tall, $250-300.

HEUBACH, ERNST, bisque socket head marked HEUBACH-KOPPELS-DORF 250 4 Germany 6; mohair wig, glass inset eyes, open mouth; mache/ wood jointed body. 23″ tall, $275-325.

HEUBACH, GEBRUDER, bisque socket head marked 8192 Germany Gebruder Heubach G H; mohair wig, glass sleep eyes, open mouth; mache/ wood jointed body. 23″ tall, $350-400.

KAMMER & REINHART, bisque socket head marked K(star)R S & H 117; human hair wig, glass flirty eyes, open mouth; mache/wood jointed body. 25″ tall, $500-550.

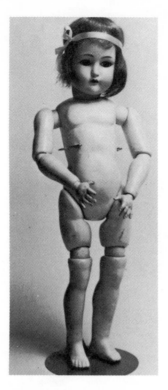

KAMMER & REINHART, bisque socket head marked K. (star) R. SIMON & HALBIG 117 58; human hair wig, glass "flirting" sleep eyes, open mouth; mache/wood jointed body. 23" tall, $550-600.

KAMMER & REINHART, bisque socket head marked K STAR R SIMON & HALBIG Germany 70; human hair wig, glass sleep eyes, open mouth; mache/wood jointed body. 28" tall, $400-450.

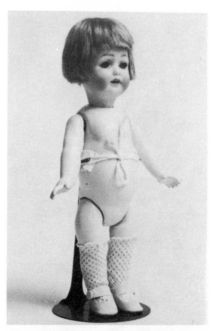

KESTNER, J. D., Jr., bisque socket head marked J made in Germany 13; mohair wig, glass sleep eyes, open mouth; mache/wood jointed body. 23" tall, $300-350.

KAMMER & REINHART, bisque socket head marked K (star) R SIMON HALBIG 121 26; human hair wig, glass sleep eyes, open mouth; mache/wood jointed body. 11½" tall, $250-300.

KESTNER, J. D., Jr., bisque socket head marked J. D. K. 260 made in Germany; mohair wig, glass sleep eyes, open mouth; mache/wood body. 8¼" tall, $225-250.

138

KESTNER, J. D., Jr., bisque shoulder head marked 154 D E P O. C made in Germany 7; mohair wig, glass sleep eyes, open mouth; kid body with bisque arms. Original costume. 13″ tall, $275-300.

KESTNER, J. D., JR., bisque socket head marked Made in G ½ Germany 7 ½ 171; human hair wig, glass sleep eyes, open mouth; mache/wood jointed body marked Germany 7½. 18″ tall, $300-350.

KESTNER, J. D., JR., bisque socket head marked K & CO. J. D. K. 260 made in Germany 62; human hair wig, glass sleep eyes, open mouth; mache/wood jointed body. 26″ tall, $400-425.

KESTNER, J. D., Jr., bisque socket head marked A made in Germany 5 152; human hair wig, glass sleep eyes, open mouth; mache/wood jointed body. 12″ tall, $300-325.

KESTNER, J. D., Jr., bisque socket head marked G½ made in Germany 7½ 164; mohair wig, inset glass eyes, open mouth; mache/wood jointed body. 18″ tall, $300-325.

MARSEILLE, ARMAND, bisque shoulder head marked A M- O -DEP Armand Marseille made in Germany; mohair wig, glass sleep eyes, open mouth; kid body with bisque arms. 21″ tall, $200-250.

KESTNER, J. D., Jr., bisque socket head marked K made in Germany 14 171; human hair wig, glass sleep eyes, open mouth; mache/wood jointed body. 27″ tall, $350-400.

MARSEILLE, ARMAND, bisque socket head marked A. 18 M.; human hair wig, glass inset eyes, open mouth; mache/wood jointed body. 42″ tall, $850-900.

MARSEILLE, ARMAND, bisque shoulder head marked 370 A M 5/0 DEP made in Germany; mohair wig, glass inset eyes, open mouth; kid body compo arms and legs. 14″ tall, $150-200.

140

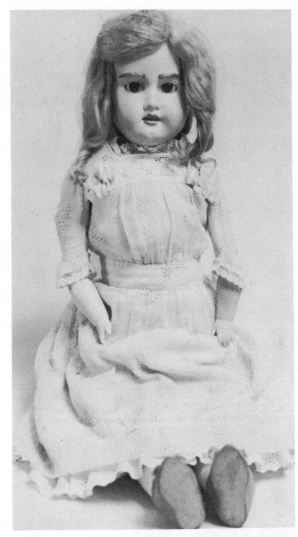

MARSEILLE, ARMAND, bisque sock-et head marked ARMAND MAR-SEILLE Germany 390 A. 6 M.; human hair wig, glass sleep eyes, open mouth; mache/wood jointed body. 23″ tall, $250-300.

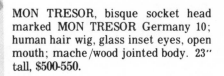

MARSEILLE, ARMAND, "FLORA-DORA," bisque shoulder head marked FLORADORA A. M. -6-DRP made in Germany; mohair wig, glass inset eyes, fur eyebrows inserted in slits in bisque, open mouth; kid body, bisque hands. 24″ tall, $275-300.

MON TRESOR, bisque socket head marked MON TRESOR Germany 10; human hair wig, glass inset eyes, open mouth; mache/wood jointed body. 23″ tall, $500-550.

RECKNAGEL, TH., bisque socket head marked R/A DEP 12/0; solid dome, mohair wig, glass inset eyes, open mouth; mache body, jointed shoulders and hips, painted shoes and socks. 8″ tall, $150-175.

RECKNAGEL, TH., bisque socket
head marked 1909 D E P R 2 A; mohair wig, glass sleep eyes, open mouth;
cardboard body with mache arms and
legs. Original costume. 18″ tall, $225-
250.

SCHMIDT, PAUL, bisque shoulder
head marked Germany P. Sch 1899 6;
human hair wig, glass inset eyes, open
mouth; kid gusseted body, bisque
hands. 22″ tall, $325-350.

SIMON & HALBIG, bisque socket head
marked S H 1078; human hair wig,
glass sleep eyes, open mouth; mache/
wood jointed body. 26″ tall, $425-450.

SIMON & HALBIG, bisque socket head
marked 12 S H 1039 D E P; human hair
wig, glass sleep eyes, open mouth;
mache/wood jointed body. 24″ tall,
$425-450.

SIMON & HALBIG, bisque shoulder
head marked 10 S H 8; human hair wig,
stationary glass eyes, open mouth;
kid/cloth body with bisque arms. 17″
tall, $350-400.

SIMON & HALBIG, bisque socket head marked S & H 1249 Germany 6½; human hair wig, glass sleep eyes, open mouth; mache/wood jointed body. 17″ tall, **each $375-400.**

SIMON & HALBIG, bisque shoulder head marked D E P 1080 - 11; human hair wig, glass sleep eyes, open mouth; kid body with bisque arms. 24″ tall, **$375-400.**

SIMON & HALBIG, bisque shoulder head marked SIMON & HALBIG 1080; mohair wig, glass inset eyes, open mouth; kid gusseted body with bisque hands. 20″ tall, **$375-400.**

SIMON & HALBIG, bisque socket head marked HALBIG K star R 50; human hair wig, glass inset eyes, closed mouth; rare all wood jointed body. 19″ tall, $450-500.

SIMON & HALBIG, "SANTA," bisque socket head marked Simon & Halbig 1249 DEP Germany SANTA 10½; human hair wig, glass sleep eyes, open mouth; mache/wood jointed body. 21½″ tall, $425-450.

UNMARKED, bisque socket head, mohair wig, inset glass eyes, closed mouth; mache jointed body. Original costume. 5½″ tall, **each $150-175.**

SIMON & HALBIG, bisque socket head marked 1249 Germany HALBIG S. & H. 13½; mohair wig, glass inset eyes, open mouth; mache/wood jointed body. 28″ tall, $450-500.

SIMON & HALBIG, "TWINS," bisque socket head marked S & H 1039 6 DEP; human hair wig, glass "flirting" sleep eyes, closed mouth; mache/wood jointed body, mama-papa pull cords. 17" tall, **pair $875-925.**

UNMARKED, bisque shoulder head; human hair wig, inset glass eyes, closed mouth; kid body with bisque arms. 19½" tall, $325-375.

UNMARKED, bisque turned shoulder head, mohair wig, glass sleep eyes, closed mouth; cloth body with bisque arms and wax-over-mache legs. 16" tall, $300-350.

WOLF, LEWIS & COMPANY, bisque
socket head marked QUEEN LOUISE;
human hair wig, glass sleep eyes, open
mouth; mache/wood jointed body. 25"
tall, $300-350.

UNMARKED, bisque socket head;
human hair wig, glass sleep eyes, open
mouth; mache/wood jointed body. 24"
tall, $325-375.

UNMARKED, (SIMON HALBIG ?),
bisque socket head; mohair wig, inset
glass eyes, closed mouth; mache/
wood jointed body. 16" tall, $475-500.

GERMAN BISQUE: Heubach figurines, piano babies

FIGURINES, unmarked, molded/painted hair, features and clothes. 9½" tall, each $260-280.

FIGURINE, unmarked, molded/painted hair, features and clothes. 8½" tall, $250-275.

FIGURINE, all bisque, sun segment mark on back; molded/painted hair, features, and clothes; intaglio eyes, open/closed mouth with upper and lower molded teeth. 5½" tall, $250-275.

PIANO BABY, unmarked; molded/painted hair, features, spectacles, top hat and clothes. 3" tall, $60-70.

PIANO BABY, unmarked; molded/painted hair, features and clothes. 1″ tall, **each $70-80.**

PIANO BABY, marked SUN with RAYS; molded/painted hair, features (intaglio eyes) and clothes. 6½″ tall, $325-350; 6″ tall, $325-350.

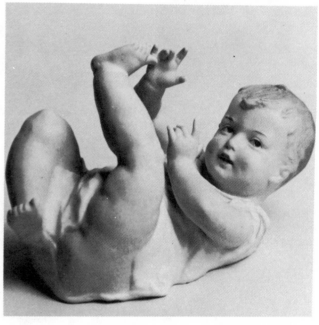

PIANO BABY, all bisque, sun segment mark on back; molded/painted hair, features, and clothes; intaglio eyes. 9″ long, $350-400.

PIANO BABY, marked SUN with RAYS; molded/painted hair, features and clothes, intaglio eyes. 8″ long, $325-350.

PIANO BABY, all bisque, sun segment mark on stomach; molded/painted hair, features, and clothes; intaglio eyes. 11″ long, $375-400.

PIANO BABY, marked 8115 Germany; molded/painted hair, features, watch and clothes. 7½″ tall, $300-325.

PIANO BABY, all bisque, unmarked; molded/painted hair, features, and clothes; intaglio eyes. 9¼″ tall, $350-375.

PIANO BABY, unmarked; molded/painted hair, features, clothes and pear; intaglio eyes. 13½″ tall, $500-550.

GERMAN BISQUE, ladies

Arranged

by manufacturer

KESTNER, "GIBSON GIRL," bisque shoulder head; original mohair wig, glass inset eyes, closed mouth; adult kid body marked (crown with streamers) J. D. K. Germany (stamped on front of torso); bisque hands. 13" tall, $2,000-2,200.

KESTNER, J. D., Jr., "Gibson Girl," bisque shoulder head marked 2/0 172 made in Germany; mohair wig, glass sleep eyes, closed mouth; cloth body with bisque arms. 15½0 tall, $2,000-2,200.

COMPANY UNIDENTIFIED, bisque socket head marked DEP 5; human hair wig, glass sleep eyes, open mouth, pierced ears; mache/wood jointed adult body marked BEBE JUMEAU Diplome d'Honneur. 19" tall, $800-850.

MARSEILLE, ARMAND, bisque socket head marked ARMAND MARSEILLE Germany 401 A7/0 M; mohair wig, glass sleep eyes, open mouth; mache/wood jointed adult body, feet shaped for high heel shoes. 13" tall, $375-400.

SIMON & HALBIG, bisque socket head marked S. & H. DEP 1159 11 Germany "WIMPERN GESETZEL SCHULTZ" (red mark inside an oval); Wimpern is German word for eyelashes; mohair wig, glass sleep eyes, open mouth; mache/wood jointed adult body. 27" tall, $550-600.

UNMARKED, bisque shoulder head; mohair wig secured through small hole in top of head; glass inset eyes, closed mouth, pierced ears; kid gusseted adult body, bisque arms. 20″ tall, $475-525.

SIMON & HALBIG, bisque shoulder head marked S 6 H 950; human hair wig, inset glass eyes, closed mouth; kid body with bisque arms. 17″ tall, $400-450.

UNMARKED, bisque solid dome turned shoulder head; mohair wig, inset glass eyes, closed mouth; cloth body with kid arms. 19½″ tall, $475-525.

UNMARKED, bisque solid dome, turned shoulder head; human hair wig, inset glass eyes, closed/mouth; cloth body with bisque arms. 25½″ tall, $650-675.

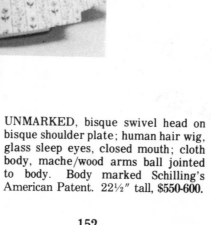

UNMARKED, bisque turned shoulder head; mohair wig, glass sleep eyes, closed mouth; cloth body with kid arms. 24″ tall, $675-700.

UNMARKED, bisque swivel head on bisque shoulder plate; human hair wig, glass sleep eyes, closed mouth; cloth body, mache/wood arms ball jointed to body. Body marked Schilling's American Patent. 22½″ tall, $550-600.

GERMAN BISQUE,
molded hair

Arranged according to date

1850-1860s TYPE, untinted bisque shoulder head, molded/painted hair, glass inset eyes, closed mouth; cloth body, bisque arms and legs. 14" tall, $475-500.

1860s TYPE, stone bisque shoulder head, unmarked, painted eyes, cloth body with bisque arms. 23½" tall, $400-425.

1860s TYPE, parian quality untinted bisque shoulder head, unmarked; painted eyes, cloth body with bisque arms. 21" tall. $525-550.

1860s TYPE, parian quality untinted bisque shoulder head; molded/painted hair, features, glazed black snood with glazed/molded white ribbon, bows on each side; pink kid body. 20" tall, $800-850.

1860s TYPE, untinted bisque shoulder head; molded/painted hair and features; cloth body with bisque arms and legs. 18½" tall, $400-450.

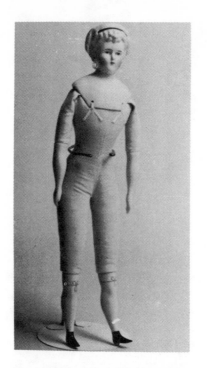

1870s TYPE, parian quality untinted bisque shoulder head with black molded bow, unmarked; painted eyes, pierced ears; cloth body with bisque arms and legs. 14½″ tall, $500-550.

1860s TYPE, bisque shoulder head; molded/painted hair and features; cloth body, kid arms. 21½″ tall, $500-550.

1870s TYPE, bisque shoulder head; molded/painted hair and features. 6½″ tall, $700-750.

1870s MAN, parian quality untinted bisque shoulder head with glazed tie and yoke, unmarked; painted eyes, kid/cloth body with kid arms. 16″ tall, $525-550.

1870s TYPE, parian quality untinted bisque shoulder head; molded/painted hair with black ribbon around bun; cloth body with kid arms. 19″ tall, $500-550.

1880s TYPE, bisque shoulder head marked H; inset glass eyes, cloth body with bisque arms and legs. 18½″ tall, $425-450.

1880s TYPE, bisque shoulder head, unmarked; painted eyes, cloth body with bisque arms. 18½″ tall, $375-400.

1880s TYPE, stone bisque shoulder head; molded/painted hair and features, molded yoke; cloth body, kid arms and legs. 17½″ tall, $400-425.

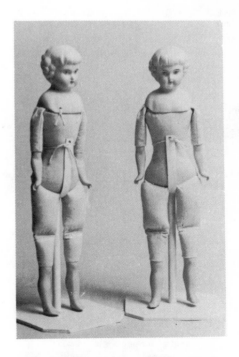

1880s TYPE, untinted bisque shoulder head, unmarked; painted eyes, cloth body with kid arms. 17½″ tall, $375-400.

1890s TYPE, bisque shoulder head, unmarked; painted eyes, cloth body with bisque arms and legs. 15″ tall, each $225-250.

1890s TYPE, stone bisque shoulder head, unmarked; painted eyes, cloth body with stone bisque arms and legs. 10″ tall, $175-200.

1890s TYPE, bisque shoulder head, unmarked; inset glass eyes, cloth body with bisque arms. 18½″ tall, $425-450.

1890s TYPE, untinted stone bisque shoulder head; molded/painted hair and features; molded/painted "Butterfly Bonnet," cloth body with stone bisque arms and legs. 8½″ tall, $275-325.

GERMAN BISQUE, Naughty Nudies

BISQUE NUDE GIRL, marked 40 V; mohair wig, molded/painted features, molded pink slippers. 3½″ tall, $125-150.

BISQUE GIRL, mohair wig, molded/painted features, molded white slippers; marked 400 L. 5″ long, $100-125.

BISQUE GIRL, mohair wig, molded/painted features, molded blue slippers, marked 405 J. 6″ long, $150-180.

BISQUE GIRL with kitten, unmarked; molded/painted hair, features and clothes. 5″ long, $130-150.

BISQUE NUDE GIRL, marked 405R; silk net over mohair wig, molded/painted features, molded pink slippers. 4″ tall, $130-160.

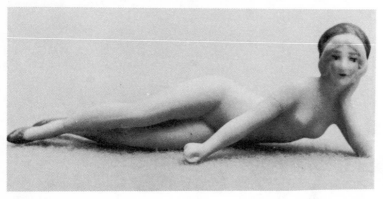

BISQUE NUDE GIRL, marked 2829 Germany; molded/painted hair, features, cap and slippers (rust). 3″ long, $75-95.

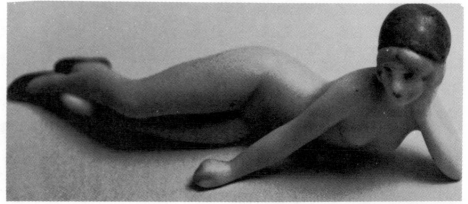

BISQUE NUDE GIRL, marked 2829 Germany; molded/painted hair, features, cap and slippers (blue). 3″ long, $75-95.

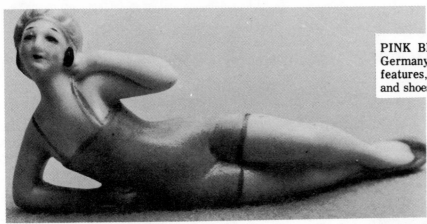

PINK BISQUE bathing girl, marked Germany 5684; molded/painted hair, features, and clothes (green cap, suit, and shoes). 3½″ long, $75-95.

PINK BISQUE bathing girl, marked Germany 5684; molded/painted hair, features and clothes (pink cap, suit, and shoes). 3½″ long, $75-95.

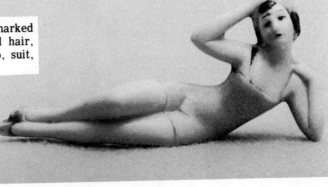

STONE BISQUE mermaid, unmarked; molded hair, features, and fins. 3¼″ long, $70-90.

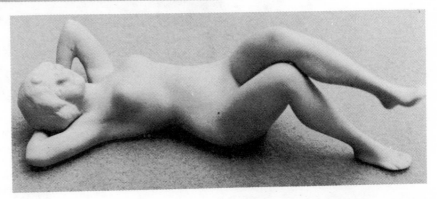

UNTINTED BISQUE NUDE GIRL (parian quality) unmarked; molded hair and features. 5½″ long, $90-100.

159

GERMAN BISQUE, Negro

SIMON & HALBIG, brown bisque socket head marked SIMON & HALBIG K STAR R made in Germany 39; mohair wig, glass inset eyes, open mouth; mache/wood jointed body. 15″ tall, $500-525.

SIMON & HALBIG, brown bisque socket head marked S 6 H 1009 DEP; mohair wig, glass inset eyes, closed mouth; brown mache/wood jointed body. 16″ tall, $525-550.

SIMON & HALBIG, brown bisque socket head marked S 3½ H 739 DEP; lamb's wool wig, inset glass eyes, open mouth; mache/wood jointed body. 11½″ tall, $350-375.

GERMAN BISQUE, Oriental

SIMON & HALBIG, olive bisque socket head marked S H 1199 Germany DEP 5½; mohair wig, glass sleep eyes, open mouth; olive color, mache/wood jointed body. 15″ tall, **$650-700.**

SIMON & HALBIG, "ORIENTAL PAIR," olive bisque socket head marked 1329 Germany SIMON & HALBIG S & H 4; human hair wig, glass inset eyes, closed mouth, pierced ears; mache/wood body jointed shoulders and hips. Original costumes. 15½″ and 16½″ tall, **pair $1,400-1,600.**

COMPANY UNIDENTIFIED, "ORIENTAL," light olive bisque head marked G/O; mohair wig, glass inset eyes, open mouth; mache/wood jointed body. All original. 10½″ tall, **$475-500.**

JAPANESE BISQUE

COMPANY UNIDENTIFIED, bisque flange head marked Made in Japan; molded/painted pigtails with bows, painted eyes, closed mouth; all cloth body. 7" long, 6½" head circumference, $55-70.

COMPANY UNIDENTIFIED, plaster-bisque head; molded/painted hair with ribbon, painted eyes, closed mouth; plaster-bisque and wood jointed body marked F H (in a diamond) Made in Japan 36 / 36. 8" tall, $65-80.

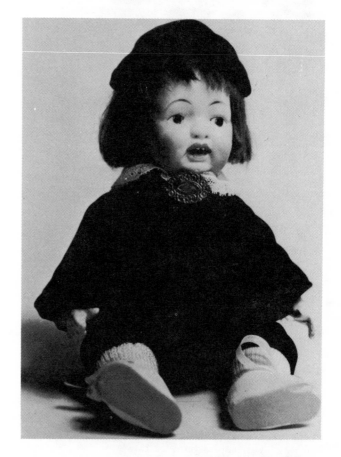

NIPPON NOVELTY COMPANY, bisque socket head marked NIPPON 3; human hair wig, painted eyes, open mouth; mache jointed baby body. 10" long, 8½" head circumference, $120-140.

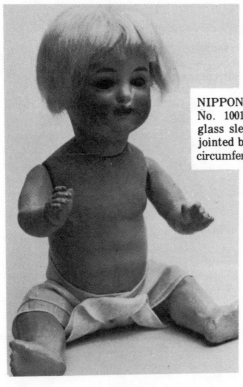

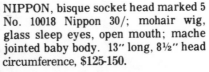

NIPPON, bisque socket head marked 5 No. 10018 Nippon 30/; mohair wig, glass sleep eyes, open mouth; mache jointed baby body. 13″ long, 8½″ head circumference, $125-150.

UNMARKED, bisque head, mohair wig, molded/painted features; wire body with bisque hands. All original. 4″ tall, $20-25.

MORIMURA BROS., bisque socket head marked 2 M B (in a circle) Japan 2/0; mohair wig, glass sleep eyes, open mouth; mache jointed baby body. 10″ long, 8″ head circumference, $125-150.

MORIMURA BROS., bisque socket head marked M B. (in a circle) Japan; human hair wig, glass sleep eyes, open mouth; mache/wood jointed body. 25½″ tall, $150-170.

MECHANICAL DOLLS

HEUBACH, mechanical music box restored to near original condition; girl, bisque socket head, mohair wig, inset glass eyes, closed mouth; mache body; boys, bisque socket head, molded/painted hair, painted intaglio eyes, closed mouth, mache body; unmarked. Music box 7" x 12"; dolls 3-5½" tall, set $3,000-3300.

COMPANY UNIDENTIFIED, MAR-OTTES, "DOLL ON STICK," (left) bisque flange head marked 1094 1; mohair wig, inset glass eyes, open mouth; double squeaker on stick body with wire to wood arms; bells, whistle on end of stick. (Right) bisque flange head marked 2/0; mohair wig, inset glass eyes, closed mouth; stick-wound music box body. All original. 15" tall (left), $325-350; 13" tall (right), $350-375.

COMPANY UNIDENTIFIED, bisque flange head marked Germany 5/0; mohair wig, inset glass eyes, open mouth; wood body (squeaker in stomach) with wire to wood arms and legs. Push stomach, head nods, hands clap cymbals. 14" tall, $400-450.

COMPANY UNIDENTIFIED, bisque flange head marked Germany 7/0; mohair wig, glass sleep eyes, open mouth; wood body (squeaker in stomach) with wire to wood arms and legs. Push stomach, eyes sleep, hands clap cymbals. All original except wig. 16" tall, $425-450.

LANTERNIER, A. & CIE, walking doll with spring wind-up cart; bisque swivel head marked MON CHERI PARIS 03 on bisque shoulder plate; human hair wig, inset pupil-less glass eyes, open/closed mouth with molded teeth; cloth body with bisque arms and metal jointed legs. 10½″ tall, $2,200-2,400.

UNMARKED MECHANICAL, mache head, human hair wig, glass eyes, closed mouth; brass body with mache arms, legs and violin; mechanism in body connected to music box. When wound head turns, eyes roll, arm with bow moves as if playing; music box plays three melodies. 18″ tall (overall), $1,200-1,400.

WOLF, LOUIS & COMPANY, "MECHANICAL," bisque socket head marked L. W. & CO. 12 11/0; mohair wig, glass inset eyes, open mouth; mache body, jointed shoulders and hips with wind key; wooden rocker rocked by flip lever. 10″ tall (overall), $675-800.

LIMOGES PEASANT CART, key wind-up boy pulls girl in cart (she shakes bells on stick); girl has bisque socket head marked S & H Germany, mohair wig, inset glass eyes, closed mouth, mache body with bisque arms; boy has bisque socket head marked Germany S & H Simon Halbig. All original. 12″ tall, $1,700-1,900.

METAL DOLLS

HELLER, ALFRED, metal shoulder head marked DIANA DEP (in a square); molded/painted hair, painted eyes, closed mouth; cloth body with bisque arms. 12½″ tall, $90-110.

JUNO (head only), metal shoulder head marked JUNO; molded/painted hair and features. 6″ tall, $65-80.

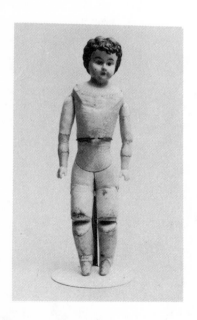

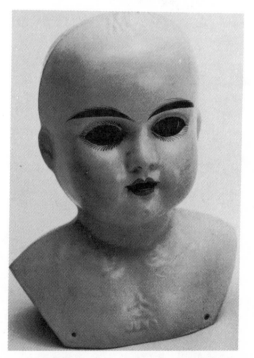

JUNO, metal shoulder head marked JUNO; molded/painted hair, painted eyes, closed mouth; kid body with bisque arms. 16½″ tall, $100-125.

MINERVA, metal shoulder head marked MINERVA Germany; molded/painted hair, painted eyes, closed mouth; all cloth body. 10″ tall, $100-125.

JUNO (head only), metal shoulder head marked JUNO; wig missing, glass sleep eyes, open mouth. 6″ tall, $90-110.

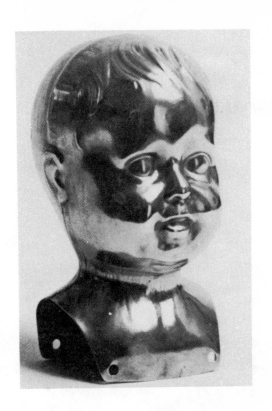

MINERVA (head only), metal shoulder head marked MINERVA Germany 4½ (a helmet); molded/painted hair, inset glass eyes, open mouth. 5″ tall, $100-125.

UNMARKED, all brass shoulder head with molded hair and features. 4½″ tall, $65-90.

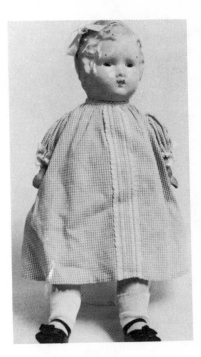

UNMARKED, metal head; molded/painted hair and features; floss wrapped body with metal hands; shoes painted blue. All original. 2¼″ long, $45-65.

VISCHER, A., & COMPANY(?), "MINERVA," tin shoulder head marked with a "helmet" on front of shoulder plate; cloth body with kid hands and shoes. 9″ tall, $75-95.

UNMARKED, metal head; molded/painted hair with slits for ribbon bow, metal sleep eyes, closed mouth, flange neck; cloth body with compo arms and legs. 20″ tall, $120-140.

167

MISCELLANEOUS MATERIALS

CORN SHUCK, corn silk hair, painted features. 9¼″ tall, $10-15.

CORN SHUCK, corn-silk hair, painted features. 9½″ tall, $10-15.

LEATHER, Moroccan leather head, hands, and feet; molded/painted features; crude cloth body marked Tangier Africa 6-10-48; baby on shoulder same. All original. 26″ tall, $150-175.

IVORY, ESKIMO, all hand-carved, painted features. Original skin clothes, primitive, museum piece. 6″ tall, $225-250.

PALMETTO (?) FIBER CLOTH, "AMERICAN SEMINOLE INDIAN," stationary head with embroidered features. Two babies same as mother. 10½″ tall, $45-60.

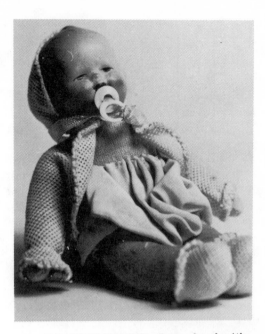

PLASTER-BISQUE, flange head with molded/painted hair and features; all cloth body. Original clothes. 5¼" tall, $25-50.

PLASTER-BISQUE, swivel head marked 463 17/0; mohair topknot, inset pupil-less glass googlie eyes, open mouth, brass rings in nose and ears and around neck; mache body jointed at hips and shoulders. Original grass skirt. 7" long, $175-200.

PLASTER-BISQUE, swivel head with molded/painted hair and features; body same material, jointed at hips and shoulders. 7" tall, each $65-80.

PORCELAIN "MICKEY MOUSE," all porcelain with molded/painted features and clothes; paper sticker, C (in circle) 1960 WALT DISNEY PRODUCTS, INC. 5" tall, $65-95.

PLASTER, "W.P.A. PROJECT DOLLS," molded plaster head, mohair wig, painted features; cotton wound, wire armature body with plaster arms and legs. All original. 9½", 15½", 16" tall, group $250-300.

RAWHIDE, AFRICAN(?), jointed at hips and shoulders, molded asphalt hair, inset bead eyes, brass ring in nostril. Primitive museum piece. 8″ tall, $250-275.

RAWHIDE, "DARROW'S RAWHIDE HEAD," molded/painted features and hair. 6¼″ tall, $250-275.

RAWHIDE, "DARROW'S RAWHIDE HEAD," molded/painted features and hair. 4½″ tall, $225-250.

SOAP, "SHIRLEY TEMPLE," all soap, unmarked; molded/painted hair and features; molded arms, legs and dress. 5½″ tall, $18-25.

TERRA COTTA shoulder head, unmarked; molded/painted hair with ribbon and bow, molded/painted features; new cloth body with bisque arms and legs. 13″ tall, $125-150.

170

PAPIER-MACHE DOLLS

COMPANY UNIDENTIFIED, mache shoulder head labeled Unbreakable Heads 6000/7; molded/painted hair, painted eyes; cloth body with kid arms. 21" tall, $250-275.

GREINER, LUDWIG, mache shoulder head labeled Greiner's improved Patent Heads Pat. March 30th '58; molded/painted hair, painted eyes; cloth body with kid arms. All original. 32" tall, $925-950.

GREINER, LUDWIG, mache shoulder head labeled Greiner's Patent Doll Heads N. 6 Pat. Mar. 30 '58. Ext. '72; molded/painted hair, painted eyes; cloth body with kid arms. 23½" tall, $300-325.

GREINER, LUDWIG, "PRE-GREINER," mache shoulder head, unmarked; molded/painted hair, inset glass pupilless eyes; cloth body with kid arms. 26" tall, $875-925.

RIDLEY, R., & SONS, mache shoulder head marked W. A. H. Nonpareil 3015; molded/painted hair and features. 6" tall, $100-125.

SUPERIOR, M & S, mache shoulder head labeled M & S SUPERIOR 2015; molded/painted hair, painted eyes; cloth body with mache arms. 20½" tall, $350-400.

SUPERIOR, M & S, mache shoulder head labeled M & S SUPERIOR ??15; molded/painted hair, painted eyes; cloth body with kid arms. 25" tall, $400-450.

UNMARKED, black mache shoulder head; mohair wig, inset pupil-less glass eyes; cloth body with mache arms and legs. 9½" tall, $325-350.

UNMARKED, early type mache/composition shoulder head; mohair wig, inset glass eyes, closed mouth; cloth body with compo arms and legs. 14" tall, $150-200.

UNMARKED, mache head in wooden cradle with squeak box. All original. 3" long, $150-175.

UNMARKED, mache head and body (one piece); molded/painted hair, molded and cloth bill cap, painted eyes; wood hands on wire arms, kid legs with molded/painted mache boots. All original. 9½" tall, $250-300.

172

UNMARKED, mache shoulder head; mohair wig, inset glass eyes; cloth body with mache arms and legs. 21″ tall, $350-400.

UNMARKED, mache shoulder head; human hair wig, inset glass eyes; cloth body with kid arms. 29″ tall, $325-350.

UNMARKED, "MILLINERS' MODEL," 1820s type, mache shoulder head; molded/painted hair and features; kid body with wood arms and legs, painted shoes. All original. 8" tall, $325-375.

UNMARKED. "MILLINERS' MODEL," 1830s type, mache shoulder head; molded/painted hair, painted eyes; kid body with wood arms and legs. 8" tall, $375-400.

UNMARKED, "MILLINERS' MODEL," 1850s type, mache shoulder head; molded/painted hair, painted eyes; kid body with wood arms and legs. All original. 8½" tall, $300-350.

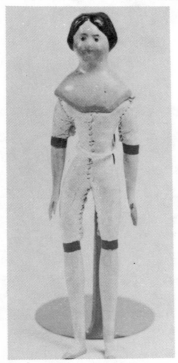

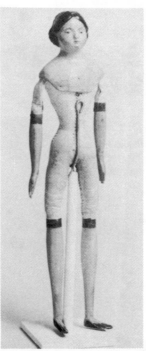

UNMARKED, "MILLINERS' MODEL," 1850s type, mache shoulder head; molded/painted hair and features kid body, painted wood arms and legs with painted shoes. 7" tall, $275-300.

UNMARKED, "MILLINERS' MODEL," 1850s type, mache shoulder head; molded/painted hair, painted eyes; kid body with wood arms and legs. 12" tall, $300-325.

PINCUSHION DOLLS

BISQUE PINCUSHION marked 938S; molded/painted hair, features, and **clothes. 2½" tall, $50-60.**

BISQUE "BABY" PINCUSHION marked 574; molded/painted hair, and features. 3" tall (overall), **$60-70.**

CHINA PINCUSHION marked Germany; molded/painted hair, features, and clothes. 3½" tall (left), $40-50. 3¼" tall (right), **$40-50.**

CHINA PINCUSHION, (left) marked Germany 16495; molded/painted hair, features, and clothes; (right) unmarked, molded/painted hair, features, and clothes. 2½" and 3" tall, **each $40-50.**

CHINA PINCUSHION, (left) marked JAPAN (ink stamp), molded/painted hair, features, and clothes; (right) marked Germany 8032, molded/painted hair, features, and clothes. 3½″ tall (left), $75-95. 4″ tall (right), $100-125.

CHINA PINCUSHION marked Germany; molded/painted hair with comb, features and clothes. 3″ tall, $140-170.

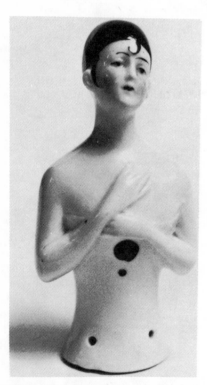

CHINA PINCUSHION marked Germany; molded/painted hair with ribbon, features and clothes. 3½″ tall, $150-175.

CHINA PINCUSHION marked 8034 Germany; molded/painted skull-cap, spit-curls, features, and clothes. 4″ tall, $150-175.

CHINA PINCUSHION marked 5979; molded/painted hair with ribbon, features, rose, and clothes. 2¾″ tall, $150-175.

CHINA PINCUSHION marked 6102
Germany; molded/painted hair with
ribbon, features and clothes. 2¾"
tall, $165-195.

CHINA PINCUSHION marked 74500
Made in Germany; molded/painted
hair, features, and clothes. 4" tall,
$175-220.

CHINA PINCUSHION marked 5230
Germany; molded/painted hair, features, and clothes. 3" tall, $175-200.

CHINA PINCUSHION, unmarked;
molded/painted hair, and features.
6" tall, $200-250.

CHINA PINCUSHION marked Germany; molded/painted spit-curls, features, and collar. 1¾″ tall, $120-150.

CHINA PINCUSHION marked Germany 2352; molded/painted hair, features, bonnet, and clothes. 3¾″ tall, $200-240.

CHINA PINCUSHION marked 5468; molded/painted hair with ribbon/flowers, and features. 2″ tall, $60-70.

CHINA PINCUSHION marked 6233 Germany; molded/painted hair with comb, features, and clothes. 3″ tall, $145-175.

CHINA PINCUSHION and powder box, unmarked; molded/painted hair, and features. 5″ tall, (overall), $95-120.

CHINA PINCUSHION marked Made in JAPAN (ink stamp); molded/painted hair, features, and clothes. 5″ tall (overall), $65-95.

CHINA PINCUSHION and powder box marked 5063 Germany; molded/painted hair, features, and clothes; box marked BRAMbilt Shoes made in Germany. 4¼″ tall (overall), $120-150.

CHINA PINCUSHION marked 1509 Germany; molded/painted cap, spit-curls, and features. 3¼″ tall (overall), $140-185.

CHINA PINCUSHION marked 9701; molded/painted hair with ribbon and comb, features, and clothes. 3″ tall (overall), $130-155.

CHINA PINCUSHION marked 10016; molded/painted hair, features (teeth and eyelids), and clothes. 6" tall, $340-380.

CHINA PINCUSHION marked JAPAN (ink stamp); molded/painted hair and features. 3½" tall, $30-40.

CHINA PINCUSHION marked Germany; molded/painted hair, features, and clothes. 2½" tall, $125-160.

CHINA PINCUSHION marked Germany 17039; molded/painted hair, features, necklace, and bracelet. 4½" tall, $230-265.

180

PAINTED BISQUE PINCUSHION
marked S1684; molded/painted hair
and features. 3½″ tall, $38-48.

PAPIER MACHE PINCUSHION
marked W (in a diamond) Germany
(ink stamp); mohair wig, painted features. 5¼″ tall, $25-35.

CHINA "Frozen Charlotte" PINCUSH-
ION, unmarked; molded/painted hair
and features; paper tag reads TEM-
PERANCE. All original. 4¼″ tall,
$140-165.

CHINA PINCUSHION marked S/685;
molded/painted hair and features. 3″
tall, $40-50.

PLASTIC and VINYL DOLLS

Arranged
by manufacturer

ALEXANDER, MADAME, "JENNY LIND," "POR-
TRETTE," all hard vinyl swivel head; synthetic wig, plastic sleep eyes, closed mouth; body marked MME. ALEX-
ANDER; jointed shoulders, hips and knees. All original.
9″ tall, $50-75.

ALEXANDER, MADAME, "GODEY," "PORTRETTE,"
all hard vinyl swivel head; synthetic wig, plastic sleep
eyes, closed mouth; body marked MME. ALEXANDER;
jointed shoulders, hips and knees. All original. 9″ tall,
$50-75.

ALEXANDER, MADAME, "AGATHA," "PORTRETTE,"
all hard vinyl swivel head; synthetic wig, plastic sleep
eyes, closed mouth; body marked MME. ALEXANDER;
jointed shoulders, hips and knees. All original. 9″ tall,
$50-75.

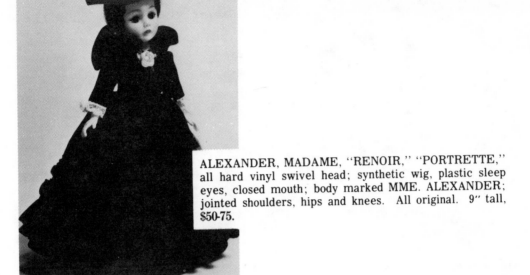

ALEXANDER, MADAME, "RENOIR," "PORTRETTE," all hard vinyl swivel head; synthetic wig, plastic sleep eyes, closed mouth; body marked MME. ALEXANDER; jointed shoulders, hips and knees. All original. 9" tall, $50-75.

ALEXANDER, MADAME, "SCARLET," "POR-TRETTE," all hard vinyl swivel head; synthetic wig, plastic sleep eyes, closed mouth; body marked MME. ALEXANDER; jointed shoulders, hips and knees. All original. 9" tall, $50-75.

ALEXANDER, MADAME, "SOUTHERN BELLE," "POR-TRETTE," all hard vinyl swivel head; synthetic wig, plastic sleep eyes, closed mouth; body marked MME. ALEXANDER; jointed shoulders, hips and knees. All original. 9" tall, $50-75.

ALEXANDER, MADAME, DIONNE QUINTS, hard vinyl swivel heads; molded/painted hair, plastic sleep eyes, open mouth with nursing hole; soft vinyl jointed baby body. All original. Tag on back of shirt—Mfg. of the "ORIGINAL QUINTUPLETS" by MADAME ALEXANDER. In original box with blanket and bottles. 7" tall, set $100-125.

ALEXANDER, MADAME, all soft vinyl, swivel head marked ALEXANDER; synthetic rooted hair, plastic sleep eyes, open/closed mouth; body jointed at shoulders only. 12½" tall, $50-75.

ALEXANDER, MADAME, EASTER DOLL, all hard vinyl, swivel head; synthetic wig, plastic sleep eyes, closed mouth; body marked ALEX (on back), jointed shoulders and hips. Only 320 dolls of this mold No. 719 were made for the Easter Season in 1968. 7¾" tall, $60-80.

ALEXANDER, MADAME, "EDITH," soft vinyl swivel head marked MME. ALEXANDER (in a circle) 1958; rooted hair, plastic sleep eyes, open/closed mouth; hard vinyl body, jointed shoulders, waist and hips. 15½" tall, $65-85.

184

ALEXANDER, MADAME, "KATHY," all soft vinyl, swivel head marked MME 1958 ALEXANDER; molded/painted hair, plastic sleep eyes, closed mouth, nursing hole; jointed baby body. All original. 16" long, 11½" head circumference, $65-85.

ALEXANDER, MADAME, hard plastic swivel head, unmarked; synthetic wig, plastic sleep eyes, closed mouth; hard plastic body, jointed at hips and shoulders, "walking" legs, turns head. 14½" tall, $65-85.

ALEXANDER, MADAME, "ELISE," all hard plastic except soft vinyl over-sleeved arms, swivel head marked ALEXANDER; synthetic wig, plastic sleep eyes, closed mouth; body marked MME. ALEXANDER; jointed shoulders, elbows, hips, knees, and ankles. All original. 16" tall, $65-85.

ALEXANDER, MADAME, "CISS-ETTE," all hard plastic swivel head, synthetic wig, plastic sleep eyes, closed mouth; body marked MME. ALEXANDER; jointed shoulders/hips above knee. 9" tall, $40-50.

ALEXANDER, MADAME, "JACQUE-LINE," vinyl swivel head marked ALEXANDER Co. 1961; rooted hair, plastic sleep eyes, closed mouth; vinyl body, jointed at hips and shoulders. 21" tall, $125-150.

ALEXANDER, MADAME, "LITTLE GENIUS," hard plastic swivel head; synthetic wig, plastic sleep eyes, open mouth/nurser; soft vinyl jointed baby body. All original with paper tag and dress label—LITTLE GENIUS by Madame Alexander. 7" long, $50-60.

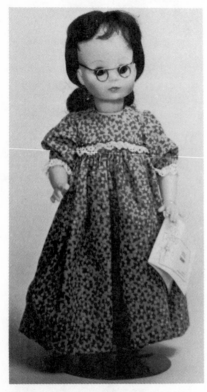

ALEXANDER, MADAME, "LITTLE GRANNY," soft vinyl swivel head marked ALEXANDER 1965; synthetic rooted hair, plastic sleep eyes, closed mouth; soft vinyl arms, hard vinyl torso and legs, jointed shoulders and hips. All original. 13" tall, $50-60.

ALEXANDER, MADAME, "LITTLE MARY SUNSHINE," soft vinyl swivel head marked ALEXANDER 1961; synthetic rooted hair, plastic sleep eyes, open/closed mouth; soft vinyl arms, hard vinyl torso and legs, jointed shoulders and hips. All original. 14" tall, $65-85.

ALEXANDER, MADAME, "MADAME DOLL," soft vinyl swivel head marked ALEXANDER 1965; rooted synthetic hair, plastic sleep eyes, closed mouth; hard vinyl body, jointed shoulders, hips and knees. All original. 14" tall, $65-85.

186

ALEXANDER, MADAME, "MARY-BEL THE DOLL THAT GETS WELL," soft vinyl swivel head marked MME. ALEXANDER (in a circle) 1962 (the 6 and 2 are reversed and the 2 is upside down); rooted hair, plastic sleep eyes, open/closed mouth; all hard vinyl body/jointed shoulders, waist, and hips. All original. 15" tall, each $65-85.

ALEXANDER, MADAME, "MARGOT," all hard plastic, swivel head; synthetic wig, plastic sleep eyes, open/closed mouth; body marked MME. ALEXANDER; jointed shoulders, hips, and knees. All original. 9" tall, $65-85.

ALEXANDER, MADAME, "ORPHAN ANNIE," soft vinyl swivel head marked ALEXANDER 1965; synthetic rooted hair, plastic sleep eyes, closed mouth; soft vinyl arms, hard vinyl torso and legs, jointed shoulders and hips. All original. 14" tall, $65-85.

ALEXANDER, MADAME, "SMARTY," vinyl swivel head marked Alexander Co. 1962; rooted hair, plastic sleep eyes, open mouth; vinyl body jointed at hips and shoulders. 12" tall, $60-70.

187

ALEXANDER, MADAME, "WENDY KIN," hard plastic swivel head, synthetic wig, plastic sleep eyes, closed mouth; hard plastic body marked ALEX. 7½" tall, $40-50.

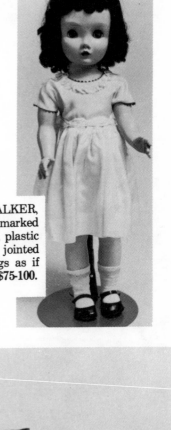

ALEXANDER, MADAME, WALKER, all hard plastic, swivel head marked ALEXANDER; synthetic wig, plastic sleep eyes, closed mouth; body jointed shoulders and hips; moves legs as if walking, head turns. 24" tall, $75-100.

ALEXANDER, MADAME, "THE TRAPP FAMILY" from *THE SOUND OF MUSIC*, (left to right) Louisa, Friedrich, Liesl, Maria, Gretl, Brigitta, Marta; soft vinyl swivel head on all marked ALEXANDER (Gretl, Marta and Friedrich are dated 1964, others 1965); all have rooted hair, plastic sleep eyes, closed mouth; arms are soft vinyl/hard vinyl torso and legs, jointed shoulders and hips. All original. 17" tall down to 11" tall, **set $250-300.**

188

ALEXANDER, MADAME, "WENDY KIN," all hard plastic swivel head; synthetic wig, plastic sleep eyes, closed mouth; body marked ALEX; jointed shoulders, hips and knees. All original. 7½" tall, $60-70.

AMERICAN CHARACTER DOLL COMPANY, "TINY TEARS," all soft vinyl, swivel head marked AMER. CHAR. INC., 19 (c in circle) 65, rooted hair, plastic sleep eyes, open closed mouth/nursing hole; jointed baby body. 17" tall, $40-50.

AMERICAN CHARACTER DOLL COMPANY, "TINY TEARS," hard plastic swivel head marked PAT. NO. 2.675.644 AME. CHARACTER; molded/painted hair, plastic sleep eyes, open/closed mouth with nursing hole; all rubber jointed baby body. Original clothes. 13" long, 11" head circumference, $70-90.

AMERICAN CHARACTER DOLL COMPANY, "TINY TEARS," hard plastic head marked AME. CHARACTER; molded/painted hair, plastic sleep eyes, open mouth; molded/jointed rubber baby body. 11″ tall, $45-65.

ARROW NOVELTY COMPANY, "SKOOKUM INDIANS," hard plastic head, mohair wig, painted eyes, closed mouth; cloth body with plastic legs and feet. 7″ tall, **pair $35-45.**

CAMEO, "KEWPIES"; (small figure) vinyl swivel head, molded/painted hair and features; vinyl body jointed at hips and shoulders; marked CAMEO; (large figure) vinyl swivel head marked 1965 JLK Co. CAMEO, molded painted hair and features; vinyl body jointed at hips and shoulders; marked Co. CAMEO. 7½″ tall, $10-20; 13″ tall, $10-20.

CAMEO, "KEWPIE," vinyl swivel head, molded/painted hair and features; vinyl body, jointed at hips and shoulders; marked CAMEO. 7″ tall, $10-20.

DELUXE TOYS COMPANY, all vinyl, swivel head marked DELUXE TOPPER 1968; rooted hair, plastic sleep eyes, closed mouth; jointed at shoulders and hips; battery operated, arms move, play tune on accordion. 18" tall, $50-60.

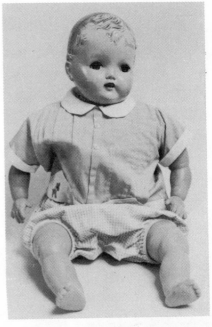

COMPANY UNIDENTIFIED, hard plastic head marked 450; deeply molded/painted hair, plastic sleep eyes, open mouth, flange neck; cloth body, voice box, soft vinyl arms and legs. 19" long, 12" head circumference, $30-40.

COMPANY UNIDENTIFIED, soft vinyl head marked MCCALL CORP. 1961 (in a circle); rooted synthetic hair, plastic sleep eyes, closed mouth; hard plastic body, arms and legs, jointed shoulders and hips. 30" tall, $45-55.

DUCHESS DOLL CORPORATION, all hard plastic, swivel head; mohair wig, plastic sleep eyes, closed mouth; body marked DUCHESS DOLL CORPORATION DESIGN COPYWRIGHT 1948 (on back); molded/painted shoes. Clothes all original. 7½" tall, $15-20.

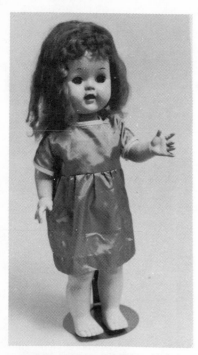

EEGEE DOLL MFG. COMPANY, WALKER, all hard plastic, swivel head, synthetic wig, plastic sleep eyes, open/closed mouth; body marked EE-GEE (on back); jointed shoulders and hips; moves legs, head turns. 17″ tall, $40-50.

EFFANBEE, "GUM DROP," all vinyl, jointed at hips and shoulders; rooted hair, plastic sleep eyes, closed mouth. Body marked EFFANBEE 1962. 15½″ tall, $20-30.

EFFANBEE DOLL COMPANY, "HONEY WALKER," all hard plastic, swivel head marked EFFANBEE; saran wig, plastic sleep eyes, closed mouth; body marked EFFANBEE (on back), jointed shoulders and hips, moves legs, head turns. 14¼″ tall, $55-70.

FRANCE, "BELLA," vinyl head; rooted hair, plastic sleep eyes, closed mouth; plastic body jointed at hips and shoulders, marked "Bella" made in France. 11½″ tall, $30-40.

FURGA, all vinyl, jointed at hips and shoulders, rooted hair, plastic sleep eyes, open mouth. Head marked FURGA/ITALY. 14″ tall, $25-35.

FURGA, "FIAMETTA," all soft vinyl, swivel head marked FURGA ITALY; rooted hair, plastic sleep eyes, open/closed mouth; body jointed shoulders and hips. All original. 14½" tall, $55-75.

FURGA, "ROSETTA," all soft vinyl, swivel head marked FURGA ITALY; rooted hair, plastic sleep eyes, open/closed mouth; body jointed shoulders and hips. All original 16" tall, $55-75.

FURGA, "TONINA," soft vinyl head marked FURGA ITALY; rooted hair, plastic sleep eyes, open/closed mouth, flange neck; pink cloth body, soft vinyl arms and legs. 16½" long, 12¼" head circumference, $40-50.

HASBRO, "G. I. JOE," all hard plastic with all human joints, molded/painted features; body marked G.I. Joe TM copyright 1964 by Hasbro Patent Pending made in USA. 11½" tall, $20-25.

IDEAL, "PEBBLES," all vinyl, jointed at hips and shoulders; rooted hair, painted eyes, open/closed mouth. Body marked Hanna-Barbera-Prod., Inc. Ideal Toy Co. Corp. F. S. 11½. 12" long, $25-30.

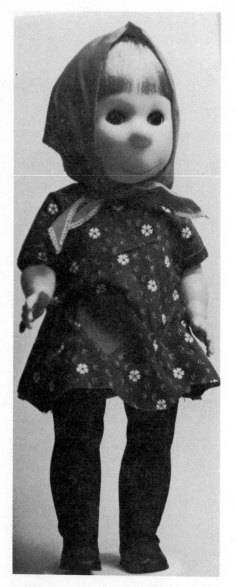

HORSMAN, "POOR PITIFUL PEARL," all vinyl, jointed at hips and shoulders, rooted hair, plastic sleep eyes, closed mouth. 18" tall, $30-40.

IDEAL, "PEBBLES & BAMBAM," all vinyl; jointed at hips and shoulders, rooted hair, painted eyes, closed mouth. Body marked Hanna-Barbera-Prod. Inc. Ideal Toy CO. Corp. F. S. 8¼ 1965. 9" long, each $18-28.

IDEAL TOY CORPORATION, "SAU-CY WALKER," hard plastic swivel head marked IDEAL DOLL W 16; nylon wig, plastic sleep eyes, open closed mouth; hard plastic body, jointed shoulders and hips; moves legs, head turns, voice box. 16" tall, $30-40.

IDEAL, "SHIRLEY TEMPLE," vinyl swivel head; rooted hair, plastic sleep eyes, open mouth; vinyl body jointed at hips and shoulders, marked S. T. 12" tall, $40-50.

IDEAL TOY CORPORATION, "KIS-SY," all soft vinyl, swivel head marked c (in circle) IDEAL TOY CORP. K-21-L; synthetic rooted hair, plastic sleep eyes, open/closed mouth; body marked c (in circle) IDEAL TOY CORP. K-22 PAT. PEND.; jointed shoulders and hips. When hands are pressed together lips pucker; hole in mouth makes kissing sound. All original in original box. 23½" tall, $45-55.

IDEAL, "TONI," all hard plastic; jointed at hips and shoulders, glued on nylon wig, plastic sleep eyes, closed mouth. Head marked P-90 IDEAL DOLL Made in USA; body marked IDEAL DOLL P-90. 14½" tall, $40-50.

IDEAL TOY CORPORATION, "SHIRLEY TEMPLE," soft vinyl, swivel head marked IDEAL DOLL ST - 12; synthetic rooted hair, plastic sleep eyes, open/closed mouth; soft vinyl torso marked (on back) ST - 14 - N; soft vinyl arms, hard vinyl legs, jointed shoulders and hips. All original. 12" tall, $35-45.

KATHE KRUSE, hard plastic head, synthetic wig, molded/painted features; cloth body with jointed shoulders and hips. Paper tag, ORIGINAL KATHE KRUSE Stoffpuppe. All original. 14½" tall, $40-50.

IRWIN PLASTICS COMPANY, all plastic, jointed at shoulders, molded/painted hair, painted eyes, closed mouth. Marked IRWIN made in USA (in a circle). 6½" tall, **pair $40-50.**

MARY HOYER DOLL MFG. COMPANY, "MARY HOYER," all hard plastic, swivel head; saran wig, plastic sleep eyes, closed mouth; body marked ORIGINAL MARY HOYER DOLL (in a circle); jointed shoulders and hips. 14" tall, $45-55.

MATTEL, "CHATTY BABY," vinyl swivel head, rooted hair, plastic sleep eyes, open mouth; vinyl body, jointed at hips and shoulders; marked Mattel 1961. 17″ tall, each $25-35.

MATTEL, "BABY FIRST STEP," battery operated walking doll; vinyl head, rooted hair, plastic sleep eyes, closed mouth; plastic body, jointed at hips and shoulders; marked Co. 1964 Mattel, Inc. Hawthorne, California made in U.S.A. U. S. Patents Pending. 18″ tall, $35-45.

MATTEL, "BUFFY AND MRS. BEASLY," (small) vinyl swivel head, rooted hair, molded/painted features; vinyl body jointed at hips and shoulders, marked 1965 Mattel Inc. JAPAN. (Large) vinyl swivel head, rooted hair, molded/painted features; vinyl body jointed at hips and shoulders, marked Co. 1967 Mattel Inc. U.S. & For. Pats. Pend. MEXICO. 6½″ tall, $8-14. 10½″ tall, $15-20.

MATTEL, "BARBIE," soft vinyl head, rooted hair, molded/painted features; jointed solid vinyl body marked Barbie Co. 1958 by Mattel Inc. Patented. "KEN"; hard vinyl head, early flocked hair wig, molded/painted features; jointed solid vinyl body marked Ken Pat. 6 Pend. MCMLX by Mattel Inc. 12″ tall, each $15-20.

MATTEL, "CHEERFUL TEARFUL,"
raising left arm changes facial expression from happy to sad; vinyl head,
rooted hair, painted eyes; mouth opens
and closes, vinyl body, jointed at
hips and shoulders. Marked Co. 1965
Mattel, Inc. Hawthorne, Cal. U.S. Patents Pending 3036-014-4. 13″ long, **each**
$20-30.

MATTEL, "CHEERFUL-TEARFUL,"
all soft vinyl; head marked 1966 MAT-
TEL INC. HONG KONG; rooted hair,
painted eyes, open/closed mouth with
nursing hole; jointed baby body. Press
stomach, mouth purses, crying expression. 6½″ long, 5½″ head circumference, $15-20.

MATTEL, "DEEDEE CUT'N BUT-
TON," vinyl swivel head, rooted hair,
molded/painted features; vinyl body
jointed at hips and shoulders; marked
Made in Japan Co. 1964 Mattel Inc.
Hawthorne, Cal. U.S.A. 15½″ tall,
$25-30.

McCALL CORPORATION, "BETSY
McCALL," hard plastic swivel head;
rooted hair on skull cap, plastic sleep
eyes, closed mouth; hard plastic body,
jointed at knees, hips and shoulders;
marked McCall Corp. 8″ tall, $30-40.

MATTEL, "SCOOTER," soft vinyl
head, rooted hair, molded/painted features; jointed solid vinyl body marked
Co. 1961 Mattel Inc. Scooter.
"RICKY"; soft vinyl head, molded/
painted hair and features; jointed
solid vinyl body marked Co. 1963
Mattel. 9½″ tall, **each** $10-15.

SHINDANA TOY COMPANY, "MA-LAIKA," ("angel" in Swahili); all brown vinyl, soft vinyl swivel head marked 44 c (in circle) 1969 SHIN-DANA TOYS DIV. OF OPERATION BOOTSTRAP INC. U.S.A.; rooted nylon hair, molded/painted features; hard vinyl body, jointed shoulders and hips. All original. 15″ tall, $25-30.

SUN RUBBER COMPANY, "MOUSE-KETEER," all soft vinyl, swivel head marked c (in circle) WALT DISNEY PROD.; molded/painted hair, plastic inset eyes, open/closed mouth; body jointed shoulders and hips; molded/painted clothes with molded/painted Mickey Mouse Club pin; molded/painted shoes and socks. 12″ tall, $25-35.

TERIGO, MARIA, "TOPO GIGIO," all molded/painted vinyl; jointed at neck and shoulders, rooted hair; marked Co. 1963 Maria Terigo. 11″ tall, $15-20.

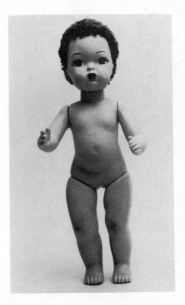

TERRI LEE, hard plastic head, synthetic wig, painted eyes, closed mouth; hard plastic body, jointed at hips and shoulders; marked TERRI LEE. 20″ tall, $60-70.

TERRI LEE, "JERRI," hard plastic head, lamb's wool wig, painted eyes, closed mouth; hard plastic body, jointed at hips and shoulders; marked TERRI LEE. 20″ tall, $60-70.

199

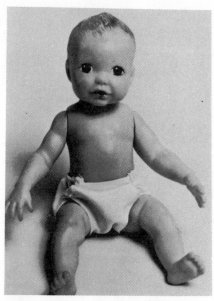

TERRI LEE, "The National Baby Sitter," all hard plastic, swivel head marked TERRI LEE; synthetic wig, molded/painted features. Receptacle in back of head to receive jack; jack and adapter assembly to be installed in record player. 16½" tall, $100-115.

TERRI LEE, "BABY LINDA," Unmarked; all soft vinyl, swivel head, molded/painted hair and features; body jointed at shoulders. 10" long, 7¼" head circumference, $10-15.

TERRI LEE, BROWN "JERRI," hard plastic head; lamb's wool wig, painted eyes, closed mouth; hard plastic body, jointed at hips and shoulders; marked TERRI LEE. 20" tall, $70-80.

TERRI LEE, "TINY TERRI LEE," "TINY JERRI LEE," walker, marked c (in circle on back); all hard plastic, swivel head, synthetic wig, plastic sleep eyes, closed mouth; body jointed shoulders and hips; head turns as legs move. 10½" tall, each $45-55.

UNEEDA DOLL COMPANY, "CO-QUETTE," vinyl swivel head marked Uneeda Doll Co. Inc. Co. 1963; rooted hair, plastic sleep eyes, closed mouth; vinyl body jointed at hips and shoulders. 16" tall, each $10-12.

UNMARKED, "CAMPBELL KIDS,"
all soft vinyl, swivel head; molded/
painted hair and features; jointed
shoulders and hips. Premium dolls,
Campbell Soup Company 1971-72. All
original. 10″ tall, **pair $15-20.**

UNMARKED, MECHANICAL, all
hard plastic; mohair wig, plastic sleep
eyes, closed mouth; body jointed shoulders and hips; winding key right side
of body, off-on lever left side; walks,
turns head, arms move up and down;
shoes have rollers on bottom. 18″ tall,
$80-90.

UNMARKED, "LINDA," soft vinyl
swivel head, rooted hair, plastic sleep
eyes, open mouth; hard vinyl torso and
legs, soft vinyl arms; hold her left
hand and she will walk. 30½″ tall,
$22-30.

UNMARKED, all hard plastic, wind-
up walking doll, turns head as she
walks; all molded/painted features
and clothes. 11″ tall, $45-50.

VOGUE DOLLS, INC., "LOVE ME
LINDA," vinyl swivel head marked
Vogue Doll Co. 1965; rooted hair, painted eyes, closed mouth; vinyl body,
jointed at hips and shoulders. 15" tall,
$25-35.

VOGUE DOLL COMPANY, "GINNY,"
walker, all hard plastic, head marked
VOGUE; mohair wig, plastic sleep
eyes, closed mouth; body marked
GINNY VOGUE DOLLS INC. PAT.
NO. 2887594 MADE IN U.S.A.; jointed
shoulders and hips, head turns when
legs move as if walking. 7½" tall,
$15-20.

RUBBER DOLLS

Arranged
by manufacturer

AMERICAN CHARACTER DOLL COMPANY, "TINY TEARS," hard plastic swivel head marked AMERICAN CHARACTER DOLL PAT. NO. 2.675.644; synthetic hair rooted in skull cap, plastic sleep eyes, open/closed mouth with nursing hole; all rubber jointed baby body. 15½" long, 13" head circumference, $35-45.

—Thomason Collection

COMPANY UNIDENTIFIED, all latex compo, swivel head marked STEHA (in an elongated diamond) DRP 839466; synthetic wig, "flirting" sleep eyes, closed mouth; jointed body and voice box. 21" tall, $55-60.

COMPANY UNIDENTIFIED, all hollow rubber with molded/painted hair, features, and clothes. Marked Made in France (in a circle). 9½" tall, $15-20.

SEIBERLING LATEX, "DOPEY," all latex marked "DOPEY" (on hat) c (in circle) WALT DISNEY SEIBERLING LATEX MADE IN AKRON, O. U.S.A. (marked on back). 5½" tall, $20-30.

SUN RUBBER COMPANY, "SO-WEE," (left) all rubber, swivel head marked SUNBABE "SO-WEE" c (in circle) RUTH E. NEWTON NEW YORK, N. Y.; molded/painted hair, plastic inset eyes, open/closed mouth with nursing hole; jointed baby body marked DESIGNED BY RUTH E. NEWTON MFD. BY THE SUN RUBBER CO. BARBERTON, O. U.S.A. PAT. 2118682 PAT. 2160739; (right) all soft vinyl, swivel head marked SUNBABE "SO-WEE" c (in circle) RUTH E. NEWTON NEW YORK, N.Y.; unjointed body marked c (in circle) THE SUN RUBBER CO. 1957. 10" long, 10" head circumference (both), each $20-30.

SUN RUBBER COMPANY, all hollow rubber with molded/painted hair, features, and clothes. Marked Ruth E. Newton The Sun Rubber Co. 8½" tall, $10-15.

UNMARKED, EARLY AMERICAN RUBBER DOLL (possibly gutta percha mixture), rubber shoulder head; molded/painted hair, painted eyes, closed mouth; cloth body with leather arms. 18" tall, $250-275.

204

WAX DOLLS

*Arranged
by manufacturer*

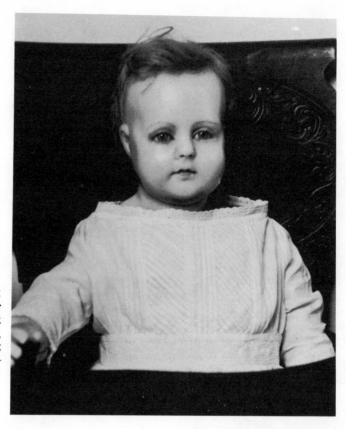

MONTANARI TYPE, poured wax shoulder head; baby fine human hair inserted in small tufts, glass inset eyes, hair eyebrows and eyelashes, closed mouth; cloth body, poured wax arms and legs. 30″ long, 14″ head circumference, $850-900.

VARGAS, all solid wax, molded wax hair, inset bead eyes, open/closed mouth; cotton clothes wax dipped. All original. 7″ tall, $125-150.

VARGAS, poured wax head; mohair wig (also beard on man), painted eyes, closed mouth; cloth body with detailed wax hands. All original. 27″ tall, **pair** $375-475.

UNMARKED, all hollow wax, painted/molded features and hair. 7″ long, $65-80.

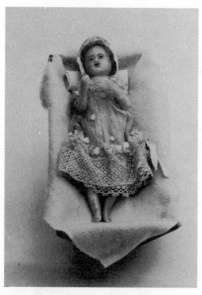

UNMARKED, solid wax shoulder head and arms (head and arms molded in one piece); mohair wig, inset pupil-less eyes, closed mouth; cloth body with solid wax legs. All original. 9" long, $150-175.

UNMARKED, NOVELTY DOLL-CANDY CONTAINER, poured wax head; inset glass eyes, bird-like fur body with metal feet; head comes off to open container. 5" tall, $100-125.

UNMARKED, FRENCH NOVELTY, poured wax baby head, arms and legs, painted features; mache egg. All original. 5¼" tall, $350-400.

UNMARKED, wax-over-mache head; mohair wig inserted in slot in head, inset pupil-less glass eyes, closed mouth; cloth, straw-stuffed body with kid arms. 15" tall, $200-250.

UNMARKED, wax-over-mache head; molded hair and ribbon, inset pupil-less glass eyes, closed mouth; cloth, straw-stuffed body with mache arms, molded/painted mache legs. 17½" tall, $200-250.

UNMARKED, wax-over-mache head; mohair wig in original setting, glass sleep eyes, closed mouth, pierced ears; cloth, straw-stuffed body with wax-over-mache arms; mache legs with molded/painted shoes. Mint condition. 17½" tall, $200-250.

WOODEN DOLLS

Arranged

by manufacturer

CANRI INC., ORTHOPEDIST, all wood, (paper label on bottom of base) TORIART ITALY 11801/6 ORTHOPEDIST ANATOMISTA ANATOM 1958 by CARNI INC. MASS.; molded/painted hair, spectacles, features, and clothes. 5½″ tall, $40-60.

COMPANY UNIDENTIFIED, "PINOCCHIO," all wood with painted features; jointed at hips and shoulders; stickers on feet read Made in Poland Pinocchio. 7½″ tall, $60-70.

HENNESSEY, WM., "TOBY," all wood, carved/painted features and clothes; 1868 Wm. HENNESSEY carved on front of body, Wm. HENNESSEY carved on back and legs. TOBY carved on hat; jointed at shoulders, tenon joints/elbows, hips and knees. 12½″ tall, $425-450.

ELLIS, JOEL, wood head (one piece with torso); molded/painted hair, painted eyes, closed mouth; wood body, tenon joints, metal hands and feet. Partially restored. 15″ tall, $650-700.

SCHOENHUT, ALBERT, wood swivel head; molded/painted hair, painted intaglio eyes, closed mouth; wood body with metal spring joints marked SCHOENHUT DOLL Pat. Jan. 17 '11, U.S.A. and Foreign Countries. 14″ tall, $425-475.

SCHOENHUT, ALBERT, wood swivel head; human hair wig, painted eyes, open/closed mouth; wood body with metal spring joints marked SCHOEN-HUT DOLL Pat. Jan. 17 '11, U.S.A and Foreign Countries. 18½" tall, $350-400.

SCHOENHUT, ALBERT, wood swivel head; mohair wig, painted intaglio eyes, closed mouth; wood body with metal spring joints marked SCHOEN-HUT DOLL Pat. Jan. 17 '11, U.S.A. and Foreign Countries. 21½" tall, $375-425.

SCHOENHUT, ALBERT, wood swivel head; mohair wig, open/closed mouth; painted eyes; wood body with metal spring joints marked SCHOENHUT DOLL Pat. Jan. 17 '11, U.S.A. and Foreign Countries. 22" tall, $325-365.

208

SCHOENHUT, ALBERT, wood swivel head; mohair wig, decal eyes, open/closed mouth; wood body with metal spring joints marked SCHOENHUT DOLL Pat. Jan. 17 '11, U.S.A. and Foreign Countries. 19½″ tall, $375-425.

SCHOENHUT, ALBERT, wood swivel head; mohair wig, decal eyes, open/closed mouth; wood body with metal spring joints; marked SCHOENHUT DOLL Pat. Jan. 17 '11, U.S.A. and Foreign Countries. 19½″ tall, $350-425.

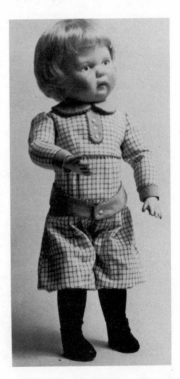

SCHOENHUT, ALBERT, wood swivel head; mohair wig, painted intaglio eyes, closed mouth; wood body with metal spring joints marked SCHOEN-HUT DOLL Pat. Jan. 17 '11, U.S.A. and Foreign Countries. 19″ tall, $375-425.

SCHOENHUT, ALBERT, wood swivel head; mohair wig, painted eyes, open/closed mouth; wood body with metal spring joints marked SCHOENHUT DOLL Pat. Jan. 17 '11, U.S.A. and Foreign Countries. 16″ tall, $300-350.

SCHOENHUT, ALBERT, "Character Toddler," wood swivel head; mohair wig, painted eyes, closed mouth; wood body with metal spring joints marked SCHOENHUT DOLL Pat. Jan 17 '11, U.S.A. and Foreign Countries. 16½″ tall, $400-475.

UNMARKED, "EARLY PEG-WOOD-EN," all wood; gesso/painted hair and features with tuck comb; peg-jointed at hips, shoulders, elbows, and knees. 2¼" tall, $175-200.

UNMARKED, CHINESE MAN, wooden head; carved/painted features, painted black hair with human hair pigtail in back, cloth body. All original. 8½" tall, $70-80.

UNMARKED, EARLY PEG-WOOD-EN, all wood, gesso/painted hair and features with tuck comb; peg-jointed at hips, shoulders, elbows, and knees. 3" tall, $200-225.

UNMARKED, EARLY PEG-WOODEN, all wood; gesso/painted hair and features with tuck comb; peg-jointed at hips, shoulders, elbows, and knees. 5½" tall (left), $240-260; 9" tall (center), $375-400; 5" tall (right), $240-260.

UNMARKED, EARLY PEG-WOODEN MAN, gesso head (one piece with torso); molded/painted hat, hair, and features; wood body peg-jointed at hips, shoulders, elbows, and knees. All original. 5½" tall, $275-300.

UNMARKED, ENGLISH PEG-WOODEN DOLLS, all wood with painted hair and features; jointed at hips, shoulders, elbows, and knees. 12½" tall, $150-175; 7½" tall, $125-150.

UNMARKED, WOODEN DOLL DRESSED AS PEDDLER, all wood with painted hair and features; jointed at hips, shoulders, elbows, and knees. 13" tall, $150-175.

DOLL PUBLICATIONS

The Doll Artisan
35 Main St.
Oneonta, NY 13820

The Dollmaker
PO Box 247
Washington, NJ 07882

Doll Castle News
PO Box 247
Washington, NJ 07882

The Doll Reader
4701 Queensbury Rd.
Riverdale, MD 20840

Collector's United
28016 Loretta
Warren, MI 48092

Bernice's Bambini
Route 2
Highland, IL 62249

Doll Talk
Box 495
Independence, MO

Doll News
(publication of United Fed. of Doll Clubs)
732 W. Lakeshore Drive
Lincoln, NEB 68528

Doll & Craft World
125 Eighth St.
Brooklyn, NY 11215

PUBLICATIONS, ANTIQUES/COLLECTIBLES

American Life Collector
Watkins Glen, NY 14891

Antique Monthly
Drawer 2
Tuscaloosa, AL 35401

Antiques
2 High St.
Wendover, Bucks,
England

Antiques
551 5th Ave.
New York, NY

Antique Trader
Dubuque, IA 52001

Antique Dealer
1115 Clifton Ave.
Clifton, NJ 07000

Hobbies
1006 S. Michigan Ave.
Chicago, IL

✓Antiques Journal
Dubuque, IA

Hobbies to Enjoy
Box 2242
St. Louis, MO 63100

✓Spinning Wheel
Hanover, PA 17331

Editor's Note:

Like everything else, subscription rates have gone up, so write for details before you subscribe. All of these publications feature articles about dolls from time to time.

DOLL/TOY MUSEUMS, U.S.A. and CANADA

ALABAMA
Meme's Dolls
955 46th St.
W. Birmingham 35208

ARIZONA
The Heard Museum
22 East Mone Vista Rd.
Phoenix 85004

Temple Historical Museum
1625 North Central St.
Temple 85282

Tombstone Courthouse
219 Toughnut St.
Tombstone 85638

CALIFORNIA
Bulah Hawkins Museum
1437 6th St.
Santa Monica 90401

First Lady Doll Collection
Buena Park 90620

Knott's Berry Farm
Buena Park 90620

Kuska Museum
24201 Walnut St.
Lomita 90717

Museum of American Treasures
1315 4th St.
National City 92050

Shirley Temple Doll Museum
4129 45th St.
San Diego 92105

Doll House Museum
40571 Lake View Dr.
Big Bear Lake 92315

Ethel Upson's Doll Museum
188 E. Main
San Jacinto 92383

California Doll & Toy Museum
932 W. 2nd St.
Benecia 94510

Ovington's Doll Land Museum
1259 East Ave. R
Palmdale 93550

Muriel's Doll House Museum
33 Canyon Lake Dr.
Port Costa 94569

COLORADO
Cameron's Doll & Carriage Museum
218 Becker's Lane
Manitow Springs 80829

Aspen Historical Society
620 W. Bleeker
Aspen 81611

DISTRICT OF COLUMBIA
D.A.R. Museum
1776 D St.
Washington 20006

National Museum
14th St. & Constitution Ave.
Washington 20560

Washington Doll's House
5235 44th St. NW
Washington 20015

CONNECTICUT
New Britain's Youth Museum
30 High St.
New Britain 06051

Memory Lane Doll & Toy Museum
Old Mystic Village
Mystic 06355

Lyme Historical Society
Lyme St.
Old Lyme 06371

Fairfield Historical Society
636 Old Post Rd.
Fairfield 06430

Madison Historical Society
853 Boston Post Rd.
Madison 06443

Meriden Historical Society
424 W. Main St.
Meriden 06450

Goshen Historical Society
Old Middle Rd.
Goshen 06756

Historical Museum,
    Gunn Memorial Library
Wykeham Rd.
Washington 06793

Stamford Historical Society
713 Bedford St.
Stamford 06901

FLORIDA
Museum of Yesterday's Toys (and Dolls)
52 St. George St.
St. Augustine 32084

Lightner Museum
King St.
St. Augustine 32084

Doll Museum
Homosassa 32646

Early American Museum
Silver Springs 32688

DeLand Museum
449 E. New York Ave.
DeLand 32720

Ruhamah's Doll Museum
2801 Beach Blvd.
St. Petersburg 33707

Wee Lassie
Doll Museum
Homestead

GEORGIA
Museum of Arts & Sciences
4182 Forsyth Rd.
Macon 31204

ILLINOIS
Dupage County Historical Museum
102 E. Wesley St.
Wheaton 60187

The Art Institute of Chicago
Michigan Ave. at Adams St.
Chicago 60603

Museum of Science & Industry
57th St. & Lakeshore Dr.
Chicago 60637

Iroquois County Historical
    Society Museum
2nd & Cherry
Watseka 60970

Lolly's Doll & Toy Museum
225 Magazine St.
Galena 61036

Time Was Village Museum
Mendota 61342

The Homestead Museum
Route 2
Clinton 61727

School of Nations Museum
Principia College
Elsah 62028

INDIANA
Countryside Doll Museum
Route 2
Salem 47167

Mother Goose Land Museum
Rural Route 1
Carlos 47329

Henry County Historical Society
614 S. 14th St.
New Castle 47374

Wayne County Historical Museum
1150 North "A" St.
Richmond 47374

Santa Claus Land
Santa Claus 47579

IOWA
Mildred Heiring Doll Museum
Highway 30
Le Grand 50142

Dept. of History & Archives
E. 12th & Grand Ave.
Des Moines 50319

Mitchell County Historical Museum
Route 4
Osage 50461

Amana Home Museum
Homestead 52236

KANSAS
Old Frontier Museum
Oskaloosa 66066

Riley County Historical Museum
11th & Poyntz Ave.
Manhattan 66502

Wichita Historical Museum Assoc.
3751 E. Douglas Ave.
Wichita 67218

Cherryvale Museum
215 E. 4th
Cherryvale 67335

KENTUCKY
Kentucky Museum
Western Kentucky Univ.
Bowling Green 42101

LOUISIANA
Louisiana State Museum
751 Chartres St.
New Orleans 70116

R.W. Norton Art Gallery
4747 Creswell Ave.
Shreveport 71106

MASSACHUSETTS
Belchertown Historical Assoc.
Maple St.
Belchertown 01007

Hardwick Historical Society
Hardwick Common
Hardwick 01037

Memorial Hall Museum
Memorial St.
Deerfield 01342

Fairbanks Doll Museum
Hall Rd.
Sturbridge 01566

Beverly Historical Society
117 Cabot St.
Beverly 01915

Historical Society of Old Newbury
98 High St.
Newburyport 01950

Wenham Historical Association
132 Main St.
Wenham 01984

Major John Bradford House
Maple St. & Landing Rd.
Kingston 02364

Hansel & Gretel Museum
Oak Bluffs 02557

Yesterdays Museum
Main & River Sts.
Sandwich 02563

Fairhaven Doll Museum
384 Alden Rd.
Fairhaven 02719

MICHIGAN
Children's Museum
67 E. Kirby
Detroit 48202

Susan's Doll Museum
18684 Beland Ave.
Detroit 48234

Montague Museum & Historical Society
Church & Meade Sts.
Montague 49437

Marquette County Historical Society
213 N. Front St.
Marquette 49855

MINNESOTA
Hennepin County Historical Society
2303 3rd Ave.
Minneapolis 55404

MISSISSIPPI
Mary Buie Museum
510 University Ave.
Oxford 38555

MISSOURI
St. Louis Historical Museum
Lydell Blvd.
St. Louis 63100

Eugene Field Museum
634 S. Broadway
St. Louis 63102

Ralph's Antique Doll Museum
7 Main St.
Parkville 64152

Society of Memories Museum
6711 Mack St.
St. Joseph 64504

Kinder Museum
Hermann 65041

Audrian County Historical Society
501 S. Muldrow
Mexico 65265

Shepherd of the Hills Museum
Branson 65616

MONTANA
Collin's Doll Museum
1601 1st Ave. S.
Great Falls 59401

NEBRASKA
Louis E. May Museum
1643 N. Nye
Fremont 68025

Johnson County Historical Society
3rd & Lincoln Sts.
Tecumseh 68450

Merrick County Historical Museum
822 C Ave.
Central City 68826

Old Brown House Doll Museum
1421 Ave. F
Gothenburg 69138

North Platte Valley Historical Assoc.
11th & J Sts.
Gering 69341

NEW HAMPSHIRE
Annie E. Woodman Institute
182-192 Central
Dover 03820

NEW JERSEY
Good Fairy Doll Museum
205 Walnut Ave.
Cranford 97016

Space Farms Museum
Beemerville Rd.
Sussex 07641

Monmouth County Historical Assoc.
70 Court St.
Freehold 07728

Morris Museum of Arts & Sciences
Normandy Hgts. & Columbia Rds.
Morristown 07960

Yesterday Museum
Morristown 07960

Raggedy Ann Antique
    Doll & Toy Museum
171 Main St.
Flemington 08822

Hope Historical Society
Hope 07844

NEW MEXICO
Gallup Museum of Indian
    Arts & Crafts
103 W. 66th Ave.
Gallup 87301

Museum of International Folk Art
Camino Lejo
Santa Fe 87501

NEW YORK
Brooklyn Children's Museum
Eastern Pkwy. at Washington Ave.
Brooklyn 10000

Cooper-Hewitt Museum
2 E. 91st St.
New York 10028

Museum of the City of New York
5th Ave. at 103rd St.
New York 10029

Aunt Len's Doll & Toy House
6 Hamilton Terrace
New York 10031

Town of Yorktown Museum
1886 Hanover Rd.
Yorktown Heights 10598

Hudson River Museum at Yonkers
511 Warburton Ave.
Yonkers 10701

Historical Society of Rockland
20 Zukor Rd.
New City 10956

Bellport-Brookhaven Museum
Bellport, Long Island 11713

Amagansett Historical Association
Main St.
Amagansett 11930

Town of Bethlehem Historical Assoc.
Clapper Rd. & Route 144
Selkirk 12158

Rensselaer County Junior Museum
282 5th Ave.
Troy 12182

The Schenectady Museum
Nott Terrace Heights
Schenectady 12308

Resnick Motor Museum
46 Canal
Ellenville 12428

The Niagara County Historical Center
215 Niagara St.
Lockport 14094

Orchard Park Historical Society
5800 Armor Rd.
Orchard Park 14127

Geneva Historical Society & Museum
543 S. Main St.
Geneva 14456

Rochester Museum & Science Center
657 East Ave.
Rochester 14603

Doll Museum
121 W. Main St.
Angelica 14709

American Life Foundation
Old Irelandville
Watkins Glen 14891

OHIO
Orange Johnson House
Worthington 43085

Milan Historical Museum
10 Edison Dr.
Milan 44846

OKLAHOMA
Eliza Cruce Hall Doll Museum
Grand at E. Northwest
Ardmore 73401

Cherokee Strip Museum
1201 Maple
Alva 73717

OREGON
Dolly Wares Doll Museum
NE Corner of 36th St.
Florence 97439

McCully House Doll Museum
5th & California St.
Jacksonville 97530

Favell Museum of Western Art
125 W. Main St.
Klamath Falls 97601

Jacksonville Free Historical Museum
Old Stage Rd.
Jacksonville 97530

PENNSYLVANIA
Pittsburgh History & Landmarks Museum
701 Allegheny Sq. W.
Pittsburgh 15212

Northampton County Historical Society
101 S. 4th St.
Easton 18042

The Happiest Angel Doll House
Newfoundland 18445

RHODE ISLAND
Rhode Island Historical Society
52 Power St.
Providence 02906

SOUTH DAKOTA
Moody County Museum
E. Pipestone Ave.
Flandreau 57028

Stuart Castle
Rockerville (near Rapid City)

TENNESSEE
Houston Antique Museum
201 High St.
Chattanooga 37403

Dulin Gallery of Art
3100 Kingston Pike
Knoxville 37919

TEXAS
Ft. Worth Museum of
    Science & History
1501 Montgomery St.
Ft. Worth 76107

White Deer Land Museum
116 S. Cuyler
Pampa 79065

Neill Museum
Fort Davis 79734

VERMONT
Farrar-Mansur House
On the Common
Weston 05161

Kent Tavern Museum
Pavilion Blvd.
Montpelier 05602

The Sheldon Art Museum
1 Park St.
Middlebury 05753

WASHINGTON
Seattle Historical Society Museum
2161 E. Hamlin St.
Seattle 98112

Museum of History & Industry
2161 E. Hamlin St.
Seattle 98112

Cowlitz County Historical Museum
Kelso 98626

Ray E. Powell Museum
212 Division
Grand View 98930

Benton County Historical Museum
Prosser 99350

WISCONSIN
Kenosha County Historical Museum
6300 3rd Ave.
Kenosha 53140

State Historical Society Museum
816 State St.
Madison 53701

Blanding House Museum of Dolls
Old Cemetery Rd.
St. Croix Falls 54024

CANADA
Bowmanville Museum
37 Silver St.
Bowmanville, Ontario

Ukrainian Arts & Crafts Museum
404 Bathurst St.
Toronto, Ontario

Yarmouth County Historical Society
Yarmouth, Nova Scotia

Editor's Note:

    We thank Mr. Gary R. Ruddell, Publisher, *The Doll Reader,* Riverdale, Maryland (subscription, $5.50 per year), for assisting us in compiling these doll/toy museums. Always write to find out when said museum, historical society, the like, is open; also, for admission fees, if any. If we have omitted a doll/toy museum, please write and tell us. And, when visiting a doll/toy museum, tell them you heard about it in the WALLACE-HOMESTEAD PRICE GUIDE TO DOLLS. Enjoy!

ABOUT THE AUTHOR

Robert W. Miller has "touched all the bases" — collector, dealer, appraiser and author of eleven books to do with antiques and collectibles; he also hosted his own television show for six years on PBS, "Antiques and Collectibles."

A former editor of The *Antique Trader Weekly,* member of the prodigious Appraisers Association of America, consultant to museums and mentioned prominently in more than twenty world-wide organizations, Mr. Miller takes just pride in the many contributions he's made in more than thirty years in the industry he loves and respects.

Mr. Miller's books are available at better book and gift stores everywhere or by writing to the Wallace-Homestead Book Company, 1912 Grand Avenue, Des Moines, Iowa 50305.